The Art of the Tart

We may live without poetry, music, and art;
We may live without conscience, and live without heart;
We may live without friends; we may live without books;
But civilized man cannot live without cooks.

Owen Meredith
(Edward Robert Bulwer, Earl of Lytton)

THE ART OF THE TART

SAVORY AND SWEET

Tamasin Day-Lewis

Photography by David Loftus

RANDOM
HOUSE

For Janie
You're my friend –

What a thing friendship is, world without end!
Robert Browning

First published in the United Kingdom in 2000 by Cassell & Co

This work was originally published in 2000 in Great Britain by Cassell & Co.

Library of Congress Cataloging-in-Publication Data

Day-Lewis, Tamasin.
    The art of the tart: savory and sweet / Tamasin Day-Lewis.
      p. cm.
    ISBN 0-375-50492-3
      1. Pies. I. Title.

  TX773 D2965 2001
641.8'652—dc21 00-032800

Design Director: David Rowley
Designed by Lucy Holmes
Typesetting by Tiger Typeset
Printed and bound in Italy

Random House website address: www.atrandom.com
98765432
First U.S. Edition

Lemon Tart (page 118)

CONTENTS

"It all starts on a kitchen chair, sleeves rolled,

with a floured, preferably marble surface, and

a wooden rolling pin. The food: the jam tart."

INTRODUCTION

There is a kind of golden age, well before entering the uncharted depths of recipe territory, when you are initiated into a fundamental rite of passage, the cooking lesson. It is the communality of the whole thing, and the complete absorption of all five senses, that make cooking one of the great seminal and sensual experiences of childhood. You watch, you listen, you smell, you copy, you taste, and, according to dexterity, height, strength, the span of attention and of those tiny hands, with the added essential ingredient of greed, the initiation is complete. And this can set you on a course that inspires a love and knowledge of food and cooking, and makes it central to your life.

It all starts on a kitchen chair, sleeves rolled, with a floured, preferably marble surface, and a wooden rolling pin. The food: the jam tart. Deep in my earliest culinary memory lies the nutty scent of dough of the crimped-edged tarts, with their bubbling lava flow of jam struggling to break through the banks and escape the crust barrier. And the unevenness of their set, your unwillingness to wait, leading to the palate-searing first mouthful, and the jam's scalding deliquescence onto the tongue. The perfect sweet-savory combination of this tiny, self-contained delicacy that you have helped to make, stretching the dough until it shrinks back at you like recalcitrant elastic, the plopping and licking of good, fruit-lumped jam from the spoon. That irresistible desire to overfill the tart shell: this time it won't burn, it won't overflow. It is as indelible a memory of childhood as puddle-jumping, smashing the upturned shell of the egg you've pretended not to eat, the soaring thrill of your first wobbly zigzag on a two-wheeler, tying a bow, writing your name.

When I decided to write a book about tarts, I looked back before I looked forward. Cooking is always about shared memory and experience, and tarts seem to have both fueled and inspired my passion for food and cooking for longer than I can remember with any reliable degree of honesty and clarity. My memories of jam tarts now are as much about my three children wonkily perched on the aforementioned kitchen chair, cuffs hopelessly scuffed with flour in their haste to cut out and roll. The corners of raw dough are eaten furtively, clumsy fingers pressing the circles asymmetrically before stickily pushing strawberry, raspberry, bramble, and apricot jam off the spoon.

The next step is unquestionably the savory sophistication of quiche Lorraine, which, ubiquitous and passé though it may seem to some, is, to my mind, when perfectly executed, with buttery pastry and an unctuously creamy, bacony, barely wobbling interior, infinitely preferable to a would-be-Provençale-ingrediented, more fashionable offering. The simple combination of thick, ivory cream, proper oak-smoked bacon, with perhaps a thin veil of Gruyère placed on it, and a butter-dotted top to glisten above a gloriously browned surface—this is food to console and please of the highest order.

Quiche goes well beyond the realms of a home economics class, though even that has been fatuously excised or sidelined at the exact point in our culinary evolution where the next generation of cooks is confronted with "heat and eat," partially cooked, ready-washed, and prepared food that bypasses completely the pleasures of cooking, and is accompanied by the mantra for our times, "fast food."

What I want to know about this culinary cul-de-sac that we appear to be going up so willingly, is what are we supposed to be saving this precious time for? And do the television cooks, food manufacturers, and supermarkets really believe in this extraordinary marketing campaign that puts speed above taste, skill, creativity, the sense of reward, and completeness one feels at having cooked a really good, if simple, meal from start to finish?

The relaxation, pleasure, enjoyment of not just preparing good food, but of eating it in the way in which it is meant to be eaten, savoring it slowly, is all the more important in the current speed-addicted climate in which we live. I find it positively insulting to be told what I haven't got time to do, and then offered a nutritionally suspect and deeply inferior alternative.

Of course, there are some foods that are delicious raw, need the minimum of preparation, are divine and quick-cooking, or, like a slow-simmered stew, a barely bubbling, somnambulant, stove-top thing, need a perfectly realistic preparation time, and can then be left to their own devices. Well, tarts are no different. My dough is made and rolled in five minutes, and its fridge time varies from nil if I'm really under pressure—I just grate freezer-cold butter into the flour—to several days. Making extra tart shells is eminently possible, as is freezing them. Then it is up to you how long you want to spend making the interior, but—being the simple yet most perfectly self-contained food that it is—it is perfectly possible to achieve in between five and 20 minutes, depending on the complexity of the filling.

The fact that we are being de-skilled, that there are actually people frightened of making dough, or who see it as a kind of Mount Everest in culinary terms, only to be scaled on high days and holidays, mystifies and distresses me.

Anyone reading this book should not doubt his or her ability to achieve every one of the recipes, and even the least experienced will know at a glance that the more time-consuming ones are not more complicated, the process is merely longer.

If you are going to cheat and skip making your own dough—and, puritan though I am, let me not be accused of being prescriptive—just make sure that it is a superior paste, and that means, for shortcrust or puff pastry, pâte sucrée or pâte sablée, ALL BUTTER. I cannot vouch for these recipes if made with an inferior crust, to my mind there is simply no point. The financial argument is marginal, too; most tarts call for 4 tablespoons of butter, which is not going to put you in the bankruptcy courts.

To Jeffrey Steingarten, too, ingredients are non-negotiable. The legendary lawyer turned food critic of *Vogue*, whom the French have honored with a Chevalier in the Order of Merit for his writing on French gastronomy, and whom I spent a day interviewing in his Manhattan loft for *Food Illustrated*, is unrepentantly firm in his belief that bad cooking is inexcusable. "Alain Ducasse makes the best tuiles. The recipe is in his book, all you have to do is look it up. Maury Rubin makes the best tart pastry. He has the City Bakery, and he's written a book. His pastry is so tender, so good. It is every baker's obligation to buy the book, or go into a different line of work if his pastry isn't as good." But here comes the crunch, the get-out clause for those who have attempted a perfectly good recipe, but without the basic wherewithal: "Technique is the hardest thing to describe. When I wrote my piece on the Ideal American Pie it ran to eight pages. I read every scientific article, and made up a foolproof recipe. It was disgusting. The scientific method didn't work."

So Jeffrey called Marion Cunningham, the doyenne of American baking, a "just beautiful" septuagenarian. "I asked her to tell me what I'd done wrong. She came and made me a pie, the best pie I've ever had. She talked, I watched. 'It's all in the fingers,' she said. I couldn't get it all in one, so I rang her and asked her to do it again, five or ten times, over the telephone as I listened and took notes. She was pleading for mercy."

I am not suggesting this as the prerequisite state of mind for dough-making, but Jeffrey's inimitable way, that of the obsessive perfectionist, is a similar if not so extreme trait in all the good cooks I know. No amount of scientific reasoning and data can substitute for the methodical care, attention to detail, technique, and impeccable ingredients that make soggy or leaden pastry an unlikely event in their kitchens.

I am not so convinced about my reader's unstraying eye or concentration to run to eight pages on the ten-step path to perfection in the construction of fine pastry. I am assuming basic skills and competence, with, perhaps, the added degree of curiosity to at least change a habit of a lifetime and try a new method.

My own methods evolve rather than change, and there is very little as satisfying, I find, as cooking something that has been one of your most well-used and well-loved recipes with a fresh eye and set of instructions. A couple of years ago I turned to Marcella Hazan's ragù recipe, and simply couldn't believe how much better it was than the one I'd thought so brilliant and cooked so often over 20 years.

A lot of the recipes in this book will, I hope, appeal on that level. These are not state-of-the-art, designer-dream, fashionable tarts. There are a few recipes that have appeared in cookbooks in one guise or another for decades, if not longer. Rather, mine, in some cases, are tweaked, pulled about a bit to reflect my approach to taste, texture, ingredients; everything one cooks makes a statement about oneself, and things like classic lemon meringue pie, treacle tart, or Bakewell tart are hardly cutting-edge cuisine, any more than is the quintessential quiche Lorraine, but these are tarts that should be remembered, celebrated, re-introduced.

I don't feel that I should have to make excuses or appear cheeky for offering recipes for some of the oldest and best-loved tarts. I remain unmoved on the subject of originality, claiming no more than that the best cooks, like magpies, pick things up along the way, petty thieves if you like, but at least they share the jewels when they discover them!

The great Jane Grigson went into print saying she believed she had created only a few truly original recipes. I admire her high-mindedness, but having learned a seemingly inexhaustible repertoire from her over the years, and on leafing through her books, as I regularly do, and still coming across untried recipes, I would rather spurn her notion of originality than agree with her. That way there is also a glimmer of hope for her successors that there is still something worth pursuing in the sharing of their recipes, and ways of cooking and eating.

The seasons play such a vital role in my cooking that recipe-testing has, like one of those lingering lunches that just doesn't end, moved imperceptibly through the furred and feathered months, through mollusks and winter roots to soft fruits and shoots, to the pink and greenery of early summer, and the hidden treasures and earthy flavors of fall, thanking God, as I perennially do, that there is no closed season for chocolate.

I am not advocating the slavish following of seasons, nor the xenophobically purist approach of only using indigenous, home-grown and -raised foods. By Christmas this year, the sight of a South American raspberry, a Peruvian fig, a South African apricot, followed by a fresh, sharp-scented Seville orange, after months of apples, pears, and dried fruits, was irresistible.

I do, however, eat in season, and from locally bred, grown, shot, or hooked ingredients most of the time. Without my own deeply inadequate supply of vegetables and herbs—which never fail to thrill when you cut, pull, or dig them yourself—augmented by a local box delivery scheme from Merricks Farm at Langport, and fish from Phil Bowditch in Taunton, including local carpet-shell clams, Brixham crabs, and wild salmon from the Tamar; without the extraordinarily dedicated and inventive Charlotte and Bill Reynolds of Swaddles Green Farm at Buckland St. Mary for organic meats and charcuterie, and the nearest—disgracefully—specialist cheese shop, Anne Marie and Tony Down's Fine Cheese Company in Bath, my food and cooking would be altogether less inspired, I would be dramatically less well informed, and my whole pleasure in planning, inventing, cooking, and eating would be far less intense.

We need a Fine Cheese Company and a Baker and Spice (see page 72) in every town; not the sempiternal horror of yet more new supermarkets carved into our countryside, further eroding choice and service, and ensuring the hearts of our towns are gutted, filleted, and half-emptied of small, original storekeepers.

Bit by bit, one is reduced to the grisly "speciality counters" of unimaginably dreary, plastic-wrapped slices of unmatured, ill-kempt cheeses; to the dubious advantages of unripenable Third World exotica; and to an erratic stocking and buying policy that left me unable to buy ground almonds, vanilla beans, or saffron one week in one of the giants. I will not name and shame. The latter two, I was informed, were too expensive. And yet there was an ill-thought-through section of ludicrously expensive honey with cherries in it, membrillo, dried porcini, and Mediterranean olive oils. How much more difficult and expensive to stock all these than, say, for each supermarket to stock the best of their regional suppliers. We have wonderful Devon and Somerset cheeses, local hard cider, a fantastic eel smoker (Brown & Forrest, at Hambridge), Rocombe Farm ice cream that puts a certain supposedly sexy rival to shame, and fantastic clotted cream.

So what is going on? The food revolution is, not surprisingly, steered but not led by the supermarkets, and it is more in their interest to invent new tubs of ready-made pasta sauce than it is, say, to build a wood-fired bakery like the one at Melmerby in Cumbria, and actually show people that the staff of life can also give you the most exciting mouthful you ever tasted. Good bread should provide a culinary framework to all our food, not be a one-off experience for those of us lucky enough to know better, be richer, live closer to the few stalwarts who have struggled to make a go of it.

It's almost funny—but not quite—that such things should be considered aspirational, treats, especially when one remembers that many tiny French villages boast a brace, not just a single boulanger and pâtissier.

I think, without doubt, there was a single defining moment when I realized that there was a complex artistry involved in the highest levels of cooking. Although hitherto unexpected, it had a profound influence, albeit not obvious at the time, on my culinary future. The year I can't remember, but I had been asked out to dinner by an ex-boyfriend and a wealthy American friend of his, who always espoused good food and female company. It was early days for Pierre Koffmann's Tante Claire, but London was aware that its culinary desert had an oasis in its midst. Royal Hospital Road was not the likeliest of places, concealed soberly and residentially from the thrum and pulse of the King's Road. There, I ate a tart that I can remember visually, and with as close to a taste memory as one can get, that has remained a nonpareil.

A delicate construction of leaf upon leaf of puff pastry, a perfectly poached pear casually gracing its summit, slightly, bitterly, caramelized, cloaking, if I am right, a whisper of a crème légère, and served with a Poires William sabayon; Koffmann's Feuilleté aux Poires was a masterpiece—I would give anything for a second helping.

Pretty early on in the conception and testing stages of this book, I realized that it would be inconceivable not to include some of the tarts that friends, cooks, and chefs I admire have invented or cooked for me.

Where I've been lucky over the past year has been in being employed to write profiles for *Food Illustrated*'s lovely editor, Neale Whitaker. What started as a one-off, we rapidly developed into a series of food-and-life-related conversations with some of the best and most original talent inside the food fraternity. Cooks, chefs, writers, restaurateurs, critics, food historians, arbiters of taste all, I have had an opportunity to talk to and, better still, in some cases to eat with a fascinating, inspiring, and generous bunch of people.

It is difficult to meet an ungenerous cook. The very heart of the experience of making food is about sharing, nurture, generosity, the giving of pleasure. When I came to sit down and write, I knew I had to include a section that I think of, provocatively, as Other People's Tarts. I don't distinguish between the accepted great and the good, and those friends of mine who I know to be exceptionally fine home cooks. Prizing the recipes off their creators has been an odyssey in itself, not through unwillingness, more from the simple reason that we all of us have more important things to do with our time, though none more so than sitting down to a good dinner. But these recipes, without exception, have constantly led me to the stove excited, curious, analytical, sometimes even hesitantly doubtful if the recipe of someone revered and respected seems to need more than fine-tuning, or a recipe that has started its life in a restaurant oven needs a complete conversion job.

The ultimate consolation has been that what started out as no more than a glimmer of an idea has managed to convince me not only that it was worth doing, but also that this most versatile and perfectly self-contained of foods is without doubt one of the great joys of my cooking life, equally as pleasurable in the making as in the eating.

Tamasin Day-Lewis

SAVORY TARTS

"Cooking is always about shared

memory and experience, and

tarts seem to have both fueled

and inspired my passion for

food and cooking for longer

than I can remember."

Potato, Garlic, and Parsley Tourte (page 26)

SOUFFLÉED CRAB TART

My local fishmonger, Phil Bowditch, gets his crabs from Brixham, and they sit, freshly boiled, and sweetly, saltily juicy, on his counter. I am rarely lazy enough to get him to dress them. I take them home, get a mallet, a hammer, and a skewer, and set to work outside on the old mill mounting block, with bits of shell and flesh flying. It seems extraordinary that in some places, the west of Ireland for one, the bodies are thrown back into the sea, the "discerning" customers wanting only the white meat of the claws. I use the deliciously rich brown meat as well as the white in this tart, which is spiked with a bit of cayenne pepper and gooily enhanced with Parmesan and Gruyère. As for the dough, I think whole wheat flour adds a deliciously complementary texture and nuttiness to the crab.

This is one of those sublime dishes, subtle yet strong, airily light yet substantial, that is perfect as an appetizer, main course, lunch, or supper. I have made a lobster version which is equally as splendid, but only in Ireland, where a neighbor's lobster-catching is not as stratospherically priced as anywhere else. If you want to try it with lobster, do; the rest of the recipe remains as is. A dish to impress and delight equally.

Serves 6

9-inch unbaked tart shell,
   chilled (page 139)
1 lb crabmeat, brown and
   white, pickled over for
   shells
salt, pepper, cayenne pepper
3 eggs, separated
1 tbsp each grated
   Parmesan and Gruyère
1 cup heavy cream
2 tsp French mustard

Preheat the oven to 400°F. Bake the tart shell blind for 10 minutes, then remove the beans, prick the bottom with a fork, and return to the oven for 5 minutes. Remove the tart shell from the oven, and turn the heat down to 375°F.

Salt and pepper the crab, going carefully with the cayenne pepper—you want a bit of heat, but nothing overwhelming.

Beat in one whole egg and two yolks, and then the cheeses, cream, and mustard. Whip the two egg whites until stiff, and fold gently and quickly into the mixture. Pour the mixture into the tart shell, and cook for about 30–40 minutes. Check after 30; it should be puffed up but have a slightly wobbly center, like a soufflé. Remove from the oven, and let cool for 10 minutes before serving.

A favorite accompaniment is a spoonful of cucumber and avocado sambal: peeled and seeded cucumber and red bell pepper chopped into tiny dice and mixed with cubes of avocado, lemon juice, olive oil, balsamic vinegar, black pepper, and finely chopped dill.

ONION TART

Precisely what the criteria are for a classic tart I cannot say—these things are all subjective—but this, like the quiche Lorraine, the flamiche, the strawberry tart, is certainly a contender. It is sweetly creamy, the onions softened to death as it were, the flavor gentle yet bold, the textures interlocking perfectly: sandy crust, soft creaminess, sticky onions.

You can muck about with the filling, adding cheese, chives, sage, thyme, anchovies, sour cream, smoked bacon, or what you will, but sometimes simplicity is the strongest suit, and for me, that is as near a definition of a classic as you can get.

A sharply dressed green salad is its ideal companion, and perhaps a glass of chilled rosé.

Serves 6
9-inch unbaked tart shell, chilled (page 139)
½ cup unsalted butter, or half butter and half olive oil
4 large onions, finely sliced
salt
4 large egg yolks
1¼ cups organic heavy cream
pepper, nutmeg

Leave the tart shell in the refrigerator while you cook the onions for the filling.

Melt the butter, or butter and olive oil, in a large, heavy-bottomed skillet, and add the onions and a pinch of salt, stirring until the onions are completely coated in the butter. Then cover the pan with a lid and cook on low heat incredibly gently until the onions are softened but not colored. Remove the lid and carry on cooking to evaporate all the liquid, stirring from time to time. This whole process will take somewhere between 40 minutes and 1 hour. Set aside to cool.

Preheat the oven to 375°F. Bake the tart shell blind for 15 minutes, then remove the beans, prick the bottom with a fork, and return to the oven for a further 5 minutes. Brush beaten egg lightly over the surface and turn the oven down to 350°F.

Beat the egg yolks with the cream, pepper, and a hint of grated nutmeg, and stir into the onions, then pour the mixture into the tart shell. Bake for about 30–40 minutes, until gently set and palely browned. Remove from the oven and let cool for at least 10 minutes before serving.

QUICHE LORRAINE

I hesitated, distrusted the strength of my feelings for this dish, until I happened upon Simon Hopkinson's eulogy to it, albeit while describing how to make a different tart altogether. I have always consigned fashionability to its rightful place, well behind taste and style and personal preference, but this dish, as I have said in my introduction, has suffered more than most since its 1960's and '70's ubiquity. The downgrading from, as it were, couture to Main Street, the demands of cheap chic in this case bastardizing both method and ingredients, mean that many people have only experienced the ready-to-wear, or in this case ready-to-eat version. And this despite the fact that its few classic ingredients and instructions ensure a creation of such consummate superiority that there is no comparison. Any more than there is between instant coffee and the real thing. So, telling it like it is is imperative.

This dish goes back at least as far as the sixteenth century. Too bad if at its half millennium it should only be known as it is popularly misapprehended.

Cream, eggs, and smoked bacon are the triumvirate, the final result dependent on the quality of this trilogy as much as on the skills of the cook. This is the real McCoy, a classic.

Serves 6

6 strips of organic smoked
    bacon
1¼ cups organic heavy cream
1 organic egg and 3 yolks
pepper

Make pie dough (page 139) with 1 cup organic white flour and 4 tablespoons unsalted butter, binding the mixture with an egg and a scant 2–3 tablespoons of water. After chilling, line an 8-inch tart pan and prick the shell with a fork. Preheat the oven to 400°F.

Snip the bacon into small strips and cook them gently in a skillet until the fat begins to run. They should remain pinkly soft, not crispened. Drain, cool slightly, then spread over the bottom of the tart shell. Whip together the cream, egg, yolks, and pepper, then pour into the tart shell, and place in the oven for 20 minutes. Turn the heat down to 350°F for a further 10–15 minutes, until the filling is goldenly puffed up like a soufflé.

Remove from the oven and let cool for 10 minutes before serving.

Souffléed Cheese Tart

This is really about turning an airy soufflé into something more substantial: strands of gooey Gruyère and salty Parmesan suspended in glossy, thick béchamel, then elevated to soufflé status with whipped egg white. Simple. A workday supper or something smarter, this is a simply delicious dish. Add a teaspoon of English mustard if you want a bit more heat. You might prefer to make the pastry with whole wheat flour.

Serves 6

9-inch unbaked tart shell, chilled (page 139)

⅔ cup milk

2 bay leaves

2 tbsp butter

¼ cup all-purpose white flour

black pepper, cayenne pepper

1 tsp English mustard (optional)

½ cup Gruyère, grated

½ cup Parmesan, grated, plus a handful for sprinkling

2 eggs, separated

1 tbsp heavy cream

Preheat the oven to 400°F. Bake the tart shell blind for 20 minutes, then remove the beans, prick the bottom with a fork, brush with beaten egg, and return to the oven for 5 minutes.

Heat the milk gently with the bay leaves. Melt the butter in a small saucepan. Add the flour and stir over a low heat for 1–2 minutes. Then whisk in the warm milk and keep stirring with the whisk over the heat until you have a thick sauce. Season with black pepper, a touch of cayenne pepper, and the mustard if you're using it. Add the Gruyère and Parmesan, then, off the heat, stir in the egg yolks whipped with a tablespoon of heavy cream. Let the mixture cool, then fold in the stiffly beaten egg whites. Pour into the tart shell, sprinkle on a handful of coarsely grated Parmesan, and cook for about 15 minutes, until puffed up, browned, and still slightly trembly. Let rest for 10 minutes before serving.

MASCARPONE AND BACON TART

Perfect for a leftover, day-before-shopping sort of supper, when the refrigerator and kitchen cabinet are contending for most empty space and inspiration is consequently at a low ebb, and subservient to a dearth of ingredients to choose from. I derive a sort of perverse satisfaction from this state of affairs, feel as spoiled by lack of choice as I do from excess of it, for, far from being an inhibitor of imagination, it is the master of it. Call it "Empty Refrigerator Tart" if you like, and if you have no bacon, prosciutto, or scraps of ham clinging to a bone, I can only suggest you go next door and borrow some, or turn to the herb tart recipe (page 51) and adapt it according to the state of your garden, your refrigerator, and the time of year.

Mascarpone, or full-fat cream cheese, works well in this plainly delicious and easy tart. Straining the cheese before you beat it into the cream and eggs ensures a beautifully smooth result.

Serves 6

6 strips of smoked bacon
or pancetta
1 cup mascarpone or
good cream cheese
a generous ⅔ cup heavy
cream
1 egg and 3 yolks
pepper

Make the dough as for Quiche Lorraine (page 18), chill, then line a 9-inch tart pan. Preheat the oven to 400°F.

Cut the bacon or pancetta into ½-inch strips and sauté gently until the fat runs. Cool slightly, then spread over the bottom of the tart shell. Whip everything else together until thick and creamily smooth, and pour into the tart shell. If the cheese is really thick you can add a tablespoon or two of whole milk to it. Cook for 20 minutes, then turn the oven down to 350°F and cook for a further 10–15 minutes, until golden brown and well risen. Remove from the oven and let rest for 10 minutes before inverting and serving.

TOMATO AND PROSCIUTTO TARTS

I seem to have temporarily forsaken the notion of serving an appetizer—most of the time. Nothing delights me more in a good restaurant, but at home there seems to be a long overdue, silent but militant consensus that when cooking for friends, we cooks want to talk to them too. The days of dinner parties where one bobs like a cork from kitchen to living room, missing punch lines and the threads of all the good conversations until the food has been cleared away, are a thing of the past. Aside from which, the protein overkill of having both meat and fish, or the sensation of being awash with soup before one starts the main course, are not something I want to feel de rigueur about. Particularly on a weekday, when a single good cheese or perhaps a glass of vin santo with cantucci to dip into it is the perfect way to end a meal.

These tarts, assembled before everyone arrives, are perfect as an ambulant appetizer. You can whip them into and out of the oven, and hand them round while people drink, without missing a beat. If you can't find good plum tomatoes, use halved organic cherry tomatoes instead.

I made a large version for an early summer lunch with 10 oz puff pastry rolled out to about 12 inches square, that just fitted my large baking sheet, and it fed six.

Makes 8 small tarts
8 slices of prosciutto,
    San Daniele if possible
⅔ cup best virgin olive oil
3 cloves of garlic
black pepper
10 plum tomatoes, or about
    40 cherry tomatoes
a handful of basil, and the
    same of either thyme
    or rosemary

Preheat the oven to 375°F. Start with 10 oz (by weight) of pure butter puff pastry dough (see page 141); this tart is characterized by its buttery, oily flakiness. Roll it out and stamp it into eight 4-inch circles, then place them on a greased baking sheet, and refrigerate until you need them.

Tear the prosciutto roughly and put it in a food processor with half the olive oil, the garlic cloves, and the pepper. Blitz for a few seconds to make a rough purée.

Slice the tomatoes, or halve if they are the cherry ones. Tear the basil leaves and add them to the remaining olive oil, but not more than 20 minutes before you are going to use them or they will bruise and blacken.

Spoon a mound of the prosciutto mixture on to each tart bottom, leaving a clear edge of about ¼ inch. Place a circle of tomatoes on top, brush with oil, sprinkle with coarsely chopped thyme or rosemary, and cook for about 15 minutes, until the dough is puffed up and cooked through. Put the tarts on a rack and brush with the basil and oil mixture, then serve them warm.

Leek, Potato, and Oatmeal Tart

Leeks and oatmeal are as much a part of Ireland's culinary heritage as praties. So I decided to combine this trinity in a tart, a wintery, substantial dish that needs nothing more than a gutsy Provençale tomato salad served alongside.

Serves 6

2 tbsp butter

the whites of 4 thick leeks, sliced ⅛-inch thick

1 garlic clove, finely chopped

salt and pepper

1 egg and 1 egg yolk

⅔ cup light cream

nutmeg

½ cup good, mature, traditionally made Cheddar (like Montgomery), grated

½ cup Parmesan, grated

3–4 medium potatoes, peeled and boiled until just tender, then finely sliced

1 tbsp fresh thyme leaves

Make your pie dough in the normal way (page 139), but use ½ cup flour and ½ cup rolled oats to 4 tablespoons unsalted butter. Chill, then roll out, and line a 9-inch tart pan, and return the pan to the refrigerator for at least 30 minutes. Preheat the oven to 375°F. Bake the tart shell blind for 10 minutes, then remove the beans, and return the tart shell to the oven for 5 minutes.

Heat the butter in a skillet and sauté the leeks and garlic gently until softened, then season them with salt and pepper. Whip together the egg, yolk and cream, seasoning with salt and pepper, adding a hint of grated nutmeg. Mix together the Cheddar and Parmesan.

Spread the leek mixture over the tart shell bottom, add a layer of potatoes, half the thyme, more salt and pepper, and half the mixed cheese, then add a second layer of potato. Pour the cream and egg mixture over the potato, and scatter the rest of the cheese and thyme over the top. Return to the oven for about 25 minutes, until the top is deliciously browned. Let cool briefly before serving.

FENNEL, TALEGGIO, AND CARDAMOM TART

This is one of those tarts that started off as a complete disaster. In my mind, the mild, subtle aniseed of Florentine fennel combined with sweet baked garlic and sharp, salty goat's cheese. I steamed and puréed the fennel, baked the garlic, and popped out a whole head of cloves like teeth out of their sockets, and, with a savory custard, added the crumbled cheese to the purée. The delicate pistachio green looked a picture, but the fennel had disappeared, overwhelmed, and the texture didn't have the requisite bite for me.

So I started all over again. This time I chose cardamom as an unobvious but possibly marriageable partner. Susan, my editor, suggested playing down the cheese and using Taleggio. The cardamom did just what it was told to do, it scented without overwhelming; the fennel took the front row, and my brother, Daniel, and his wife, Rebecca, were the guinea pigs for a late, light Monday lunch. We were all delighted with the result, which we demolished with watercress and red chard salad dressed with walnut oil, olive oil, and cider vinegar.

Serves 6

9-inch unbaked tart shell, chilled (page 139)
4 bulbs fennel
2 tbsp butter
4 tbsp each olive oil, white wine, and water
the crushed seeds of 8 cardamom pods
2 heaping tbsp crème fraîche
2 eggs and 2 egg yolks
1 cup heavy cream
about 1 cup whole milk
salt and pepper
⅓ cup Taleggio

Preheat the oven to 375°F. Bake the tart shell blind for 15 minutes, then remove the beans, prick the bottom with a fork, and return to the oven for 5 minutes.

Remove all the tough outer layers of the fennel, then quarter the bulbs, and slice thickly. Put the fennel into a heavy-bottomed skillet with the butter, olive oil, wine, water, and cardamom seeds. Bring to bubbling, reduce to simmering, cover with a lid, and cook gently until the fennel is no longer resistant even at the core, about 10–15 minutes. Remove it with a slotted spoon, reserve, and bubble the juices until stickily reduced and syrupy, about 2–3 tablespoons.

Whip together the crème fraîche, eggs, and yolks with enough cream and milk to bring a pitcherful of the savory custard to almost 2½ cups. Add the fennel liquor to the custard mixture and beat together thoroughly. Season with salt and pepper.

Cube the Taleggio into small squares. Spread the fennel over the tart shell, then scatter the Taleggio over it. Pour on the custard and bake until barely set and browned, about 25 minutes. Eat warm.

Potato, Garlic, and Parsley Tourte

Strictly speaking, a tourte is not a tart, but, since some tarts have a double crust, and since this is irresistibly delicious, it demands to be included.

Before you decide not to make it because you can't be bothered to make puff pastry, let me tell you what I did last week. I rang Baker and Spice (see page 72) and put in an order. For £16.50 (about $32) I bought 2.2 pounds of puff pastry, all butter. Now, given that that is enough for four tarts, or a tourte and two large tarts, and that it saves a morning rolling and turning and folding and cursing, this seems like a great value, and a corner that you can legitimately cut. I don't live round the corner, but I do carry my tray-sized flat parcel of puff pastry home to Somerset on the backseat of the car when I get the urge.

Puffed up and golden, with a flood of garlic-scented cream bubbling under its lid, this is a refined but hearty winter dish served on its own, but on Sunday I decided to accompany it with tarragon roast chicken, browned parsnips, and carrots Vichy. I cooked it as I do my tatins, in a Le Creuset skillet, the kind with a short, enameled, ovenproof handle.

Serves 6 – 8

just over 1 lb potatoes,
 sliced very finely
3 garlic cloves, finely
 chopped
3 tbsp finely chopped
 flat-leaf parsley
salt, pepper, nutmeg
1 beaten egg
 and 2 egg yolks
1 cup organic heavy cream

Preheat the oven to 400°F. You will need 14 oz (by weight) puff pastry, and to roll out two circles, one larger than the other. Grease your skillet or gratin dish, and line with the larger pastry circle.

In a large bowl, mix the potatoes—which must be sliced very finely, or they will not cook through before the crust is perfect—together with the garlic, parsley, and seasoning. Layer them into your skillet or dish, then cover with the puff pastry lid, sealing the edges with a fork, and brushing the top with beaten egg. Cut a cross in the middle of the lid for the steam to escape, and bake for 50 minutes.

Whip the egg yolks and cream together, remove the pie from the oven, and, with a tiny funnel held in the steam hole, pour in the eggy cream. Please pour slowly, or you'll get a geyser of cream that will then lie on top of your crust. I know, it happened to me the first time around, and with a larger funnel! If you would rather, you can delicately run the tip of a knife blade around the crust and gently lever the lid up to pour in the cream.

Return to the oven for 10 minutes, then serve the flaky triangular wedges hot from the pan.

Tomato, Goat's Camembert, and Herb Tart

This is an utterly compulsive late spring/early summer tart, when the herbs in my garden are flowering and as intensely flavored as the goat's Camembert. The cheese is melting, yet doesn't surrender its shape, and the strong counterbalance of Gruyère and mustard take this tart well out of the orbit of the ordinary. I would serve it any time, any place, anywhere; it oozes rustic sophistication, and is utterly unlike the eggy, creamy dishes we think of when we think of savory tarts. If you have time, make your herbed brushing oil the night before, so that the flavors have time to marry.

*Serves 6 for supper,
8 for lunch*

1 tbsp Dijon mustard
¾ cup Gruyère, grated
1 dozen or so organic
    tomatoes, sliced
¼ lb Camembert-style goat's
    cheese (such as mature
    Coach Farm Cheese), sliced

Herbed brushing oil

½ cup extra virgin olive oil
2 tsp each finely chopped
    rosemary, thyme,
    basil, fennel, and
    flat-leaf parsley
1 garlic clove, crushed
salt and pepper
1 bay leaf

Combine all the ingredients for the brushing oil in a jar or bowl and leave overnight, if possible, or at least for a couple of hours.

Make pie dough (page 139) with 1½ cups organic white flour and 5½ tablespoons unsalted butter, but use good olive oil instead of water—you might need a bit more than 2 tablespoons. Chill, then roll, and line a 12-inch tart pan.

Preheat the oven to 375°F and put a baking sheet in the oven.

Spread the mustard over the tart shell bottom, then scatter over the Gruyère. Cover with alternate overlapping layers of tomato and goat's cheese in concentric circles, then brush two-thirds of the herby oil over the surface. Bake the tart on the preheated baking sheet for about 35 minutes; it will be heaving, brown, and bubbling. Remove from the oven, brush with the remaining oil, and let cool for at least 10 minutes before inverting and serving.

Fava bean and asparagus salad would dress it up, a simple green one would dress it down.

FLAMICHE

A classic Northern French tart, which can also be made with galette yeast dough (see page 104), or covered with a second tier of pastry and turned into a more substantial pie. The scent of leeks sweating gently, sweetly, in butter is one of the great kitchen smells, subsiding as they do into a collective mess that is all buttery white purée. The addition of ham, bacon, pancetta, while fine if that is what you feel like, takes away from the purity of the flamiche, which is all about leeks, butter, and cream, period! Use only the firm, inner white core of the leeks. Keep your color for the side, say some of the new leaves that are on the market now—red chard, mustard, tat soi, bok choy—with a grainy mustard dressing to instill a sharp note.

Serves 6
9-inch unbaked tart shell, chilled (page 139)
3 lbs leeks
6 tbsp unsalted butter
⅔–1¼ cups organic heavy cream
3 egg yolks
salt, pepper, nutmeg

This tart is not baked blind, so allow time for your leeks to cool before spreading the wilted, white heap on the crust.

Trim off the coarse, green outer leaves of the leeks and chop the white parts into roughly ½-inch rings. Sauté them slowly over low heat in about 6 tablespoons butter until they are thoroughly softened: start checking after 20 minutes; it might take 30. Let them cool.

Preheat the oven to 350°F. Whip together the cream and egg yolks, and season with salt, pepper, and a hint of grated nutmeg. Stir this into the leeks, and spread the mixture quickly and evenly over the tart shell bottom. Cook for 35–40 minutes, until tremblingly set. Leave for 10 minutes before inverting and serving.

I think this is good cold, too, on a picnic, although if you gauge it right and wrap it up tightly in tinfoil, it is perfection barely tepid on a cold Irish beach.

CHARD, GRUYÈRE, AND CRÈME FRAÎCHE TART

Swiss chard has a kind of mild, crunchy earthiness which needs gentle enhancing rather than masking, but it adds good texture and flavor, and the virtue of being somehow unexpected.

I found some wonderfully squat bunches with thick, wide, flat white ribs and racing green, shiny, squeaky leaves in a lovely shop called Dandelion on the Wandsworth / Clapham border in London. My great friend Janie and I had been tramping across the common on a particularly grisly, drizzly March day, on a quest for some good soup and vegetables for a late lunch. Dandelion provided both, and I decided that gooey-sharp Gruyère, crème fraîche, and the blanched white ribs of chard would make a delicious tart.

Serves 6
9-inch unbaked tart shell, chilled (page 139)
2 heads of Swiss chard
1 cup of organic crème fraîche
4–6 tbsp whole milk
1 egg and 4 egg yolks
¾ cup Gruyère, grated
¼ tsp cayenne pepper
salt and pepper

Preheat the oven to 400°F.

Strip the leaves off the chard, and wash leaves and ribs carefully. Then slice the ribs rather like you would celery, to about ½-inch widthwise, and steam them until tender. Drain and let cool.

Bake the tart shell blind for 15 minutes, then remove the beans, prick the bottom with a fork, brush with beaten egg, and return to the oven for 5 minutes. Turn the oven down to 350°F.

Beat the crème fraîche, milk, egg, and yolks together until smooth, then stir in the cheese and cayenne pepper, and, sparingly, some salt and pepper.

Quickly assemble the layer of cooled chard ribs on the tart bottom, pour over the custard, and cook until browned, about 30 minutes. I served mine with the steamed chard leaves with a spritz of lemon and black pepper, and some gingery glazed carrots.

SORREL TART

The lemony-sharp flavor of sorrel in hollandaise, soup, sauce, is always a foil to the richness of eggs, cream, butter. It is also less frequented territory than the ubiquitous spinach that people usually grow alongside it. A row of its yellowy green leaves, shooting up like a weed, is all you need, but if you don't grow it, it is widely available. Its tartness here, reminiscent of the astringence of rhubarb, with which it shares the constituent oxalic acid, is assuaged by the sweetness of the onions.

Serves 6
9-inch unbaked tart shell, chilled (page 139)
¾ lb sorrel, washed and stemmed
4 tbsp unsalted butter
¾ lb onions, finely sliced
2 eggs and 2 yolks
1½ cups organic heavy cream
salt and pepper

Preheat the oven to 375°F. Bake the tart shell blind for 15 minutes, then remove the beans, prick the pastry all over with a fork, and return to the oven for a further 5 minutes. Remove from the oven and brush with beaten egg.

Throw the sorrel into a saucepan full of boiling salted water, and take it out and drain it the moment it comes back up to a boil. The leaves will be an unappetizing grayish color, but don't let that put you off. Stew them in 2 tablespoons of the butter until all their liquid has evaporated, and they have wilted down into a purée; this will take about 20 minutes. Do likewise with the onions in a separate pan, which will take a bit longer, keeping them covered, and occasionally giving them a stir. They should not brown, but be meltingly translucent, a pale tangle.

Mix the onions with the sorrel in a bowl, and when tepid, stir in the whipped eggs and yolks, cream, and seasoning. Pour this into the tart shell and cook for about 35–40 minutes, until barely set and barely colored. Let cool for at least 10 minutes before inverting and serving.

PORCINI MUSHROOM AND RED ONION TART

This is a wonderfully intense, musky flavored tart, perfect for the lean, wintery months when one turns more to the kitchen cabinet and to dried foods than at any other time of year. The mascarpone, delicately enhanced by the Porcini liquor, makes it less rich than if it was full of cream, and it doesn't set in quite the same way as the eggier tarts; rather it slides slowly off its tart shell bottom when sliced, like an earthy, densely flavored ragout. This makes an exquisite and original appetizer.

*Serves 10 as an appetizer,
6 as a main course*

¾ cup dried porcini
   mushrooms
2 medium-sized red onions
2 tbsp unsalted butter
1⅛ cups mascarpone
1 large egg and 3 yolks
8–10 sage leaves, or
   2–3 sprigs of thyme
salt and pepper

Soak the porcini mushrooms in 1½ cups of warm water for about an hour, turning them when you remember, to ensure they're all completely rehydrated.

Meanwhile, make pie dough (page 139) with 1 cup whole wheat or organic white flour—a wholewheat crust is always delicious with mushrooms. Chill, then roll out, and line a 9-inch tart pan—or a rectangular pan measuring 14 x 5 inches. Preheat the oven to 400°F. Bake the tart shell blind for 10 minutes, then remove the beans, prick the bottom with a fork, and return to the oven for 5 minutes. Remove from the oven and brush the tart shell with a little beaten egg. Turn the oven down to 350°F.

Strain the mushrooms, pressing gently, and reserve the liquid. Slice the onions finely into rings, and sauté them gently in butter for a few minutes until they're softened. Chop the mushrooms coarsely and add them to the onions, cooking them for a few more minutes. Strain the mushroom liquid into the pan and let it reduce completely, then tip the mixture into a bowl and let it cool. You can complete the cooking to this stage several hours before if it is more convenient.

Whip the mascarpone, egg, and yolks together, then add the finely chopped sage or thyme, and stir the mushroom and onion mixture into it. Season with salt and pepper, then spread the mixture over the bottom of the tart shell, and cook for 10 minutes. Turn the heat down to 325°F and cook for a further 25–30 minutes. Check it after 25, to see quite how loose it is. Remove from the oven, still obviously shuddery, and let cool for 10 minutes before inverting and eating it warm.

L'Aligot Tart

I write this in some trepidation. I know for sure it will not meet with the approval of Simon Hopkinson, although it is a rare occasion when he doesn't see eye to eye with Elizabeth David. In her classic French Provincial Cooking, *Elizabeth David writes about l'*aligot, *a country dish that she came across at Entraygues, "a little town on the confluence of two rivers, the Lot and the Truyère, in south-western France." Floury potatoes, butter, cream, salt, and garlic, and tomme de Cantal, a soft, white unfermented local cheese, are the ingredients, but Mrs. David suggests that in the absence of tomme de Cantal, which is not a great traveler, and should not be eaten when more than three or four days old, one can substitute the mild, easily melting Caerphilly, or an unmatured Lancashire, of which a little less, as it is stronger flavored. Simon Hopkinson is adamant: "I strongly disagree." He travels to Michel Bras's restaurant in Laguiole in the Auvergne, and enjoys his authentic l'*aligot *as part of a two-starred lunch.*

Well, I still haven't experienced the real thing, but I know of the affinity between potatoes, garlic, and cheese, and I can promise you that a combination of the most melting of Italian cheeses, Fontina, and crumbled Caerphilly, makes a delicious and robustly filling tart.

Make a larger-than-you-need quantity of the filling, and you can turn the remainder into potato cakes, flouring them lightly, and frying them in butter until crustily bronzed.

Serves 6

9-inch unbaked tart shell, chilled (page 139)
about 2 lbs floury potatoes
salt and pepper
about ⅔ cup light cream
4 tbsp unsalted butter
1 garlic clove, crushed
¼ lb each Fontina and Caerphilly, cut into small dice

Preheat the oven to 400°F. Bake the tart shell blind for 20 minutes, then remove the beans, prick the crust with a fork, brush with beaten egg, and return to the oven for 5 minutes.

Meanwhile, cook the potatoes in their skins, then peel them and mash them thoroughly with some salt and pepper. Heat the cream and butter together in a saucepan, then mix with the mashed potatoes, stirring vigorously with a wooden spoon. Add the garlic and the diced cheeses and stir until well amalgamated.

Turn the oven down to 325°F. Fill the tart shell with the potato mixture, and cook the tart for about 20 minutes. Let cool for 10 minutes before inverting and serving.

SMOKED BACON AND GARLIC TART

Sweet, soft heads of garlic, oiled, wrapped, and baked in their skins, are a delicious contrast to the fat, smoky strips of juicy bacon, these two heavier notes lifted with the fresh taste and verdant color of chopped parsley. Do not blench at the garlic; blanch. The quantity of garlic might imply dragon's breath, but the blanching part—in this case, the virtual steaming of the little buds sealed like bodies in a sauna—ameliorates, sweetens, makes mild of this ferocious bulb. Even more so when the new season's garlic comes in.

Virgil said that garlic is the right food to maintain the strength of harvest reapers. I don't think the modern equivalent would complain of lack of substance if confronted by this dish.

Serves 6

9-inch unbaked tart shell, chilled (page 139)

3 heads of garlic

3 tbsp olive oil

3 strips of oak-smoked organic bacon, or about ¼ lb of cooked, smoked ham

2 tbsp chopped flat-leaf parsley

1 egg and 2 yolks

½ cup each organic heavy cream and whole milk

Preheat the oven to 400°F. Bake the tart shell blind for 15 minutes, then remove the beans, prick the bottom with a fork, brush with beaten egg, and return to the oven for 5 minutes.

Put each head of garlic on a square of tinfoil that will scrunch up tightly and seal it in, dribbling over a spoonful of olive oil before you wrap it up. Put them in a roasting pan and bake until soft. Test with a skewer after 25 minutes.

Snip the bacon into small strips and cook gently in a skillet until the fat runs. If using cooked ham, sauté it in a little butter. Turn off the heat, throw in the parsley, so it is coated in the bacon fat. Unwrap the garlic and pop each bud out onto a plate.

Whip together the egg, yolks, cream, and milk. Put the garlic, bacon, and parsley into the bottom of the tart shell, then pour in the custard and bake for about 25 minutes. Remove from the oven and let cool for about 10 minutes before inverting and serving.

MONKFISH TART WITH BÉARNAISE

Serves 6 as a main course, or makes 10 – 12 small tarts

9-inch unbaked tart shell, or ten to twelve tartlets, chilled (page 139)
about 1 lb monkfish, skinned and sliced
salt and pepper
butter
4 cups chanterelles or organic mushrooms, cleaned and chopped
a handful of tarragon

Béarnaise sauce
2 tbsp tarragon vinegar
1 shallot, finely chopped
3 tsp finely chopped tarragon
⅔ cup unsalted butter
2 egg yolks

This can be made either as one whole tart, or as little tarts that need just a last-minute assembly job before serving with drinks, an ambulant appetizer. They need only 5 minutes in the oven, and everything can be prepared in advance. Monkfish is tenderly, juicily fleshy, so there is no chance of the tarts drying out. If you can get wild mushrooms for the base, do, chanterelles particularly; if not, some organic mushrooms will do fine.

Preheat the oven to 400°F. Bake the tart shell blind for 20 minutes if it is a large tart, 10 minutes if small, then remove the beans, prick the bottom with a fork, and brush with beaten egg before returning to the oven, for 10 or 5 minutes respectively. The crust should be crisp and cooked. Turn the heat up to 425°F.

Season the slices of fish and sauté them in a generous chunk of butter on both sides until just opaque. Remove the fish from the pan and add the mushrooms, cooking them until they are completely softened.

Make the béarnaise by heating together the tarragon vinegar, shallot, and 1 teaspoon of the chopped tarragon in a small stainless steel saucepan, until the liquid has almost all evaporated. Melt the butter in a small saucepan and let settle for a minute or two. Remove the vinegar mixture from the heat, add the egg yolks, and whip until thick. Then, little by little, very slowly pour in the hot melted butter, leaving behind the white residue, whipping as you go. Strain the sauce and scatter in another 2 teaspoons of chopped tarragon.

Put a layer of mushrooms in the tart shell, followed by the slices of monkfish, then pour over the béarnaise. Sprinkle on a bit more tarragon, and put the tart or tarts in the oven for a quick blast of heat: 5 minutes is all they need. Serve at once.

BRANDADE TART

I first ate brandade de morue in Provence, unsurprisingly, where it is something of a national dish. The morning markets in the glorious towns of Apt, Cavaillon, Carpentras, and l'Isle-sur-la-Sorgue, where the summer heat filters down through huge plane trees and all life is brighter, slower, more headily scented, are the places to buy it. Huge, dirty cream triangles hung out to dry like old, bald sheepskin rugs, their curious fishy salt smell hanging in the air; you point, you insist on a piece from the middle, not the tail—the bottom handkerchief corner is more salt, less succulence—and then you conceal your purchase, like well-ripened cheese, from well-honed nostrils while you lunch in a market-side restaurant. Then you take it home and launder it like sheets, in several changes of water, for a good 24 hours.

Classically, it is accompanied by bread fried in olive oil and strong black olives. This is a dish the southern French traditionally serve on religious festival days, at Easter and Christmas, but it is great all year round, and translates well into tart format. Make sure you use your best olive oil.

Serves 6 as a main course, or makes 10–12 small tarts

9-inch unbaked tart shell, or ten to twelve tartlets, chilled (page 139)
1 large potato, about ¼ lb, peeled
1 lb chunk of salt cod, soaked in several changes of water for at least 24 hours, then drained
⅔–1¼ cups cold pressed olive oil
⅔–1¼ cups whole milk
3 garlic cloves
1 lemon
black pepper
Provençal black olives and some flat-leaf parsley

Prebake your tart shell or shells completely for this dish as for the monkfish tart on page 39; they will need only a final 5-minute fling in the oven.

Steam the potato in chunks until cooked, then mash or put it through the coarse blade of a mouli-légumes.

Run your fingers over the soaked cod and use tweezers to pull out any bones. Either put the fish in a saucepan of cold water, bring to a boil, switch off instantly, and leave for a few minutes, or pour boiling water over it to cover and let it soak for 10–15 minutes, until a fork can flake it without resistance.

Warm the olive oil in a saucepan and do likewise with the milk and garlic in another pan. Skin the cod and put it in chunks into a food processor, switch on, and pour in the olive oil and milk alternately, in a slow, steady stream. You can either add or discard the garlic. When you have a thick paste, invert it into a bowl, and stir in the mashed potato with a wooden spoon. Add the juice of up to the whole lemon, to taste, and black pepper. You won't need salt. Invert into the tart shell or shells, return to the oven for 5 minutes, then decorate with the olives and parsley, and serve warm.

SCALLOP, ARTICHOKE, AND SMOKED BACON TART

January. The leanest month. But there are fat, sweet scallops, and earthily misshapen artichokes, twisted knobbly roots that are a peeler's nightmare, but worth every knuckle-grating minute. This combination, a dark-dayed inspiration, is one I would even go so far as to say I was proud of, and, unusually, it was perfect first time round. A seriously special tart.

Serves 6–8

9-inch unbaked tart shell, chilled (page 139)

⅓ lb Jerusalem artichokes

6 large scallops, cleaned, with the whites separated from the corals

4 strips of smoked bacon

1¼ cups heavy cream

3 tbsp whole milk

2 eggs and 2 egg yolks

salt and pepper

Keep the tart shell in the refrigerator while you prepare the filling. Preheat the oven to 375°F.

Peel the artichokes and slice them into thin coins, ⅛-inch thick. Steam until tender, then let cool. Slice the whites of the scallops into three discs each, and the corals into two if they are large-sized. Snip the bacon into thin pieces and sauté in its own fat until really crispy. Drain and dry on paper towels.

Line the tart shell with the cooled artichokes, then cover with a layer of the raw scallops, distributing them evenly, then dot with the bacon.

Whip the cream, milk, and eggs together, season with salt and pepper, and pour gently from a pitcher so as not to displace the filling ingredients. Cook for 35–40 minutes; the corals will stick out of the top in their deliciously gaudy-colored way, and be just cooked. Let cool for 10 minutes, then invert, and serve with a mustardy-dressed plain green salad.

Smoked Haddock and Watercress Tart

Watercress is every bit as much a player as spinach with smoked haddock, the iron-rich peppery leaves cutting the sweet smokiness. This is a wonderful everyday tart loved by everyone in my family.

Serves 6

9-inch unbaked tart shell, chilled (page 139)

¾ lb undyed smoked haddock

1¼ cups whole milk

2 tbsp butter

1 small onion, finely chopped

1 celery stalk, finely chopped

¼ cup white flour

salt, pepper, nutmeg

a bunch of watercress (stalks removed), finely chopped

2 eggs, beaten

2 tbsp grated Parmesan

Preheat the oven to 375°F. Bake the tart shell blind for 10 minutes, then remove the beans, prick the bottom with a fork, and brush with beaten egg. Return to the oven for a further 5 minutes.

Put the haddock and milk in a saucepan and bring to a boil, then reduce the heat and simmer for a further 10 minutes. Skin the fish and flake into a bowl. Reserve the milk separately.

Heat the butter in a saucepan, add the onion and celery, and cook gently until softened. Stir in the flour and cook for a couple of minutes, then add the reserved poaching milk, and stir until the sauce has thickened. Season with a little salt, pepper, and grated nutmeg. Remove from the heat and stir into the fish, adding the watercress and beaten eggs. Pour into the tart shell and sprinkle the top with the grated Parmesan. Bake in the oven for 25–30 minutes, when the tart will have risen and be crusted a delectable golden brown. Let cool slightly before inverting and eating hot.

Spinach and Anchovy Tart

Perfect at any time of year, but plus perfect in the spring, when you can buy or grow tiny pousse, the baby leaves of spinach that are gently, tenderly unferrous, and don't exude copious amounts of liquid when you cook them. Spinach and anchovies: what can I say, other than that they are a heavenly marriage, and, inspired by a soufflé, I set out to reproduce the taste in a tart. Curiously, there is no battle, therefore no winner, no loser between these two strong tastes when they're set in conjunction; the one doesn't cancel out the other, but enhances it. Just don't be tempted to add more anchovies than I've used in the recipe below, and don't add salt: the anchovies have it in spadefuls.

Serves 6
2 tbsp unsalted butter
1 tbsp olive oil
¾ lb organic baby spinach
black pepper
1 cup heavy cream
1 egg and 2 yolks
12 anchovy fillets

Make your pie dough (page 139) with 1 cup organic white flour and 4 tablespoons unsalted butter, but, instead of adding water, add a generous tablespoon of your best olive oil to the mixture before blitzing it all together. Chill, then roll out, and line a 9-inch tart pan. Preheat the oven to 375°F. Bake the tart shell blind for 15 minutes, then remove the beans, prick the bottom with a fork, and return to the oven for a further 5 minutes.

While the tart shell is in the oven, heat the butter and olive oil in a heavy-bottomed enamel saucepan, add the spinach and black pepper, and stir briefly until it has wilted but not lost its shape, about a couple of minutes.

Whip the cream, egg, and yolks together, then pour in any liquid from the spinach pan. Tip the spinach and anchovies into a food processor and process briefly, keeping their texture and not reducing them to a slushy purée. Throw them into the bowl with the cream and eggs, and whip together, then pour the whole thing into the tart shell in the oven and cook for about 25 minutes.

Let cool for 10 minutes, then serve with something plain, like cherry tomato salad, and good, white country bread and butter, as I did for lunch this May Day Saturday.

ASPARAGUS TART

As soon as the first tender shoots of Evesham asparagus appear, I am done for. First I eat mounds of them, bare but for the best unsalted butter dribbled extravagantly over them, and a grinding of coarse pepper. Then there comes a point where I can begin to bear sharing their flavor with others, not using them as the star turn. A dish of late spring vegetables, perhaps, fresh peas, fava beans, asparagus, and shallots brought together at the last moment, buttered and minted; a salad of asparagus, broiled red bell peppers, and the thinnest sliced raw fennel, red and green, cooked and raw combined in a lemony dressing; or an asparagus tart, all green spears and creaminess, tender, juicy, almost mellow.

Never, never think you can squeeze more out of each fragile wand than you really can. By that, I mean always chop every stem to where it starts feeling woody, and peel the lowest inch or two just to be safe. I tend to chop the wands into generous 1-inch lengths, with the spears longer by their spear-head, so to speak. Then, golden rule, which I try never to short-cut, steam the chopped stems for a few minutes before you throw the tender buds in after them; that way you won't get the flobby mess that putting them in together can lead to. The point of a sharp knife should pierce the flesh firmly but unresistantly. Then stop cooking immediately. One fat bundle of asparagus will fill your tart shell. I think Parmesan is a great enhancer here, but you could be a purist and rest with cream and eggs.

Serves 6

9-inch unbaked tart shell,
  chilled (page 139)
1 good–sized bundle
  of asparagus
1¼ cups cream
⅔ cup whole milk
4 egg yolks
2 tbsp freshly grated
  Parmesan
salt and pepper

Preheat the oven to 400°F. Bake the tart shell blind for 15 minutes, then remove the beans, prick the bottom with a fork, and return to the oven for 5 minutes. Remove the tart shell from the oven and brush with beaten egg. Turn the oven down to 350°F.

Steam your asparagus as discussed in the introduction. Whip the cream, milk, and egg yolks together, add the grated Parmesan, and season with salt and pepper. Spoon the cooled asparagus into the tart shell, then pour over the custard. Cook for 25–30 minutes, until puffed up and just set and browned.

Let cool for 10 minutes, then invert, and serve with a strong-noted salad, say raw fennel, orange, and watercress with walnut or hazelnut and olive oil dressing, which introduces astringence and pepperiness.

ZUCCHINI AND BASIL TART
WITH RAW TOMATO DRESSING

The mild, fugitive flavor of the zucchini flees altogether if it is introduced to water, but, curiously, is brought out by the strongest of tastes. Think of ratatouille—where it finds its place perfectly—of basil, tomato, garlic, Parmesan, green olive oil, or tarragon, which would substitute beautifully for the basil here.

The zucchini have to be small, green-fingered, and squeaky firm, the flowers just off them, for me to bother with. Once they're puffed up and waterily bloated, the insides like wet wood pulp, I don't want to know.

I don't put Parmesan or Gruyère in this tart, although they are perfect in a gratin of zucchini; I think they would overwhelm it. If you don't like the idea of fresh tomato dressing, you could make simple mozzarella di bufala and tomato salad to serve at its side.

Serves 6

9-inch unbaked tart shell,
  chilled (page 139)
1¾ lbs small, firm zucchini
2–3 tbsp olive oil
2 eggs and 2 yolks
¾–1¼ cups heavy cream
salt and pepper
a handful of sweet basil
  leaves (about 4 tbsp)

Tomato dressing

1 small onion
1 garlic clove
1½ lbs tomatoes, peeled,
  seeded, and finely chopped
6 tbsp olive oil
1 tbsp each torn basil
  leaves, chopped chives,
  and flat-leaf parsley
2 tbsp lemon juice
salt and pepper

Preheat the oven to 375°F. Bake the tart shell blind for 15 minutes, then remove the beans, prick the bottom with a fork, and return to the oven for 5 minutes.

Slice the zucchini into thinnish coins and layer them in a colander, salting each layer. Let drain for 20–30 minutes, then rinse, and dry on paper towels.

Heat the olive oil in a large, heavy-bottomed skillet, throw in the zucchini, and cook until they are slightly softened and translucent, but do not allow them to color. Remove from the pan and drain.

Whip together the eggs, yolks, cream, and seasoning. Put the zucchini into the tart shell with the torn basil, and pour over the egg and cream mixture. Bake until just set, puffed up, and deliciously browned, about 30 minutes. Let cool for about 10 minutes before inverting, and eat while warm with the gutsy raw tomato dressing, made while the tart is in the oven.

For the dressing, mince the onion and garlic together in a food processor. Put in a bowl with the remaining ingredients, stir, then cover and refrigerate for 20 minutes. Stir again, and spoon onto the plates alongside the tart.

TOMATO AND SAFFRON TART

When I first saw a recipe for tomato and saffron quiche in Simon Hopkinson's lovely book Ham and Spinach, *with the gently cajoling statement that it came a close second to his favorite quiche from Lorraine, it didn't take me long to get to work. The cut tart is as brazenly primary-colored as you could hope for, with its sunset stripes of scarlet and yellow, and with, I think, one of the smoothest, most soothing of saffrony custards imaginable. The texture is ambrosial.*

Like all tinkerers, I decided to change a few details, largely at the behest of my oldest daughter, Miranda, whose critical faculties when it comes to judging tarts are nothing short of lethal. She demanded that I make it with the tomato-sauce base that I use in my tomato and oatmeal tart, stating that the tinniness and texture of the tomatoes was not quite right. This is going to make more than double what you need, but I never see the point in making small quantities of fresh tomato sauce: it keeps well in the refrigerator for several days, or you can freeze it. Use it with cod, meatballs, pasta, or what you will. Of course, adjust the quantity if you want to.

Serves 6

9-inch unbaked tart shell,
    chilled (page 139)
1¾ cups heavy cream
1 tsp saffron threads,
    steeped in 1 tbsp hot
    water for 5–10 minutes
2 eggs and 4 egg yolks
1 dozen basil leaves
salt and pepper

Fresh tomato sauce

3 tbsp olive oil
2 onions, 2 celery stalks,
    6 garlic cloves, finely
    chopped
2¼ lbs ripe tomatoes,
    peeled, seeded, and
    chopped

Preheat the oven to 400°F. Bake the tart shell blind for 15 minutes, then remove the beans, brush the pastry all over with beaten egg, and return to the oven for 10 minutes. Remove from the oven and let cool. Turn the heat down to 325°F and put a large baking sheet into the oven.

For the tomato sauce, heat the oil in a large, heavy-bottomed skillet, and sauté the onions, celery, and garlic until softened and translucent. Add the fresh and canned tomatoes, which you can chop once they're in the pan. Add the passata, the paste, bay leaves, and sugar, then the red wine, and keep at a steady simmer for at least 30 minutes, until the sauce is thick, and the liquid evaporated.

You can either use it as it is, or, which I prefer, put it through the largest setting of your mouli-légumes to make a coarsely textured purée with enough bite to complement the heavenly, trembly custard that comes to rest on it. Let cool while you make the custard.

Put 4 tablespoons of the cream in a small saucepan with the saffron threads and their water. Heat until warm, then let infuse for 5 minutes. Beat together the eggs and yolks, and stir in the remaining cream and the saffron cream. Do this with a

1 x 14 oz can Italian plum
  tomatoes, organic
  if possible
1 cup organic tomato
  passata (strained
  tomatoes)
1 tbsp tomato paste
2 bay leaves
2 tsp brown sugar
⅔ cup red wine
salt and pepper

fork: saffron threads wrap themselves around a whisk. Tear the basil into small pieces, stir it into the custard, and season with salt and pepper.

Spread a layer of the tomato mixture over the shell, to come almost halfway up the tart shell. Put the tart with its tomato layer onto the heated baking sheet, on a rack slightly pulled out of the oven, then carefully pour in the saffron custard from a pitcher. Bake until tremblingly set—about 30–40 minutes—and an intense, goldy color with brown patches. Let cool for at least 10 minutes before inverting and eating.

Thinly sliced raw fennel salad, coated in a dressing of the best olive oil with a squeeze of lemon juice, is the only other thing you'll need.

TOMATO, THYME, AND PARMESAN TART

There was a day, not so long ago, when vegetarianism meant nut cutlets, socks-and-sandals, and sprouting mung beans. Lentil bake sat drying and crusting round the edges in wholefood restaurants, alongside earthy, solid, unrelieved plates of fiber, to which the words enjoyment, cuisine, were somehow strangers, unrelated. The food was too busy being good for you.

That even our best chefs and cooks now offer genuinely inventive vegetarian food, with no obvious sense of its being enforced tokenism, is as it should be. We flesh eaters can all be vegetarians on our nights off, and the socks-and-sandals brigade can smarten up their act, and serve us something we might actually want to eat.

This tart is enough to convert even the most recidivist of meat and two veggers. It is one of the greats, a classic of vegetarian cooking. I have served it at a "big girls' lunch" and had everyone begging for the recipe. You could, of course, make this with regular pie dough, but the sturdier oatmeal crust makes it perfect for picnics.

Serves 8—10
1 organic egg
⅔ cup heavy cream
1 tbsp each Parmesan and
    Gruyère, grated
2 tbsp mature Cheddar,
    grated
fresh thyme

Tomato sauce
See page 48. You might like
    to add 1 tbsp each fresh
    thyme, flat-leaf parsley,
    and basil

Make pie dough in the normal way (page 139), but use 1 cup organic white flour, 1 cup organic porridge oats, and ½ cup unsalted butter. Chill, then roll out, just a little thicker than for normal pie dough and line a 12-inch greased tart pan. Reserve the remaining dough in strips for a lattice or, if you can't be bothered, save it for another tart shell. Preheat the oven to 375°F. Bake the tart blind for 10 minutes, then remove the beans, prick the bottom with a fork, and return to the oven for 5 minutes.

Make the tomato sauce as on page 48; if you like, you could reverse the proportions of fresh and canned tomatoes. Add the thyme and parsley with the bay leaves, and simmer, uncovered, until the sauce is beginning to thicken, stirring occasionally for about 15 minutes. Add a good splash of wine, season, and simmer for another 30 minutes or so, giving it the odd stir, and adding a bit more wine if it dries out. Sprinkle with the torn basil when it has cooled down a bit.

Whip the egg and cream together, then whip in the Parmesan, Gruyère, and half the Cheddar. Season and scatter in a bit of thyme. Spread a thick layer of tomato sauce over the bottom to come halfway up the tart shell, then pour over the custard, and arrange your pastry lattice over the top. Bake for about 25 minutes, until set and palely browned. Let cool for about 10 minutes before serving.

HERB TART

This tart is either brilliant by design—in late spring when all the herbs are rushing with growth and intensely flavored—or when the cupboard is bare, and all you can find are the basics: eggs, cream, milk, and flour, and whatever you've got growing in your herb garden. Any combination of the ones listed below makes a good tart, and a thrifty dinner.

Serves 6

9-inch unbaked tart shell, chilled (page 139)

2 tbsp unsalted butter

1 heaping tbsp each flat-leaf parsley, tarragon, basil, thyme, chives, and chervil

2 eggs and 2 yolks

2 cups heavy cream, or half cream and half whole milk

salt, pepper, nutmeg

1 cup Gruyère or Emmenthal, grated

2 tbsp coarsely grated Parmesan (optional)

Preheat the oven to 375°F. Bake the tart shell blind for 15 minutes, then remove the beans, prick the bottom with a fork, and return to the oven for 5 minutes. Brush with beaten egg and let cool.

Heat the butter in a skillet, add the herbs, and stir briefly to coat. In a large bowl, whip together the eggs, yolks, and cream, or cream and milk, season with salt and pepper, including a hint of grated nutmeg, then stir in the grated Gruyère or Emmenthal. Stir in the herbs, then pour the mixture into the tart shell, and cook for about 25   30 minutes. After about 15 minutes you can sprinkle over a couple of tablespoons of coarsely grated Parmesan if you like a cheesier flavor. Let cool for about 10 minutes before serving.

Brown Onion and Basil Pissaladière

This makes a wonderful summer lunch, a tangle of onions browned in balsamic vinegar and spicy green globe basil, with giant Napoletana basil torn over the tomato topping. Of course, use ordinary basil if that's all you can find.

Serves 5–6

For the dough

2¼ cups organic pasta flour

6 tbsp butter

2 eggs

1 cake compressed yeast

salt

For the topping

olive oil

just under 2 lbs organic onions, thinly sliced

2 tbsp of the best balsamic vinegar

2 heaping tsp brown sugar

a good handful of basil

salt and pepper

2 x 2 oz cans of anchovies, drained

4 new garlic cloves

6 organic tomatoes, peeled

I made my dough in the food processor with the dough hook, but it is easy by hand. Sift the flour, add the butter in small pieces, and process briefly, or rub in using your fingertips. Make a well in the center, and add the eggs, the yeast dissolved in 4–5 tablespoons of tepid water, and a pinch of salt. Process until it comes away from the bowl in a ball. (If making the dough by hand, mix the eggs and yeast with the flour, gradually drawing the flour in from around the edge of the well, then knead lightly until the dough comes together.) Put it on a floured plate, cover with a floured cloth, and put somewhere warm for 2 hours.

For the topping, heat a few tablespoons of olive oil in a large, heavy-bottomed skillet, add the onions, and cook gently until translucent. Add the balsamic vinegar, brown sugar, a handful of basil leaves (green globe basil if you can get it, but in any case keeping a few leaves back to scatter over the top when it comes out of the oven), and salt and pepper. Stir until glossily browned all over, then cover the pan and leave it, but for the occasional stir, for 30 minutes. Pound the anchovies with the peeled garlic cloves.

Preheat the oven to 375°F. After 2 hours the dough will have doubled in size. Punch it back, knead it briefly, then put it in the middle of an olive-oiled baking sheet, about 14 x 9 inches. Press the dough out with your knuckles to cover the sheet, spread the onion mixture evenly over the surface, then the anchovy mixture, and let rise for a further 15 minutes. Cook in the center of the oven for 20 minutes, then turn down the oven to 350°F and cook for a further 15–20 minutes. Remove from the oven, lay slices of peeled raw tomatoes and torn basil over the top—this is where I have used giant Napoletana basil, when I have been able to get hold of it—dribble over a little olive oil, slice, and eat hot-and-cold in your fingers.

CORN AND SCALLION TART WITH A POLENTA CRUST

You can of course make this tart with ordinary pie dough, but this crust is a stunning yellow color with the corn's characteristic slight grittiness, and, with the fresh corn cobs, it is doubly corny! The milky sweetness of fresh, plump buds of corn is not quite enough on its own, so I gently sautéed some scallions in butter, and the tart's essential mildness had a counterpoint. This really is a good dish on a day when you want something wholesome without being aggressive-tasting. Early fall is obviously the natural time for it, when the first small cobs of corn are at their tenderly sweetest, sheltering kernels that are spurting with milk.

Serves 6

1 cup organic quick-cooking
    polenta
add sea salt
2 bunches of scallions (outer
    skins removed), finely
    chopped
a pat of butter
2 eggs and 2 yolks
1¼ cups heavy cream
2 corn cobs, cooked, with
    the kernels stripped off
    the cobs onto a plate
salt, pepper, cayenne pepper

Preheat the oven to 350°F.

For the polenta (cornmeal) crust, simply bring 1 cup of water to a boil in a saucepan and slowly pour in the polenta. Throw a pinch of sea salt after it, and stir over gentle heat for 5 minutes. Remove from the heat and form the polenta into a ball. Using a bit of flour—not polenta, which would make the finished crust gritty—roll out in the normal way to line a 9-inch tart pan, remembering that, unlike flour-based dough, this is good-tempered enough to be pressed into the pan if it breaks anywhere. Prick the bottom and bake in the preheated oven for 10 minutes. You don't need to bake it blind with beans.

Sauté the scallions in the butter until softened and translucent, then add them into the whipped eggs, yolks, and cream, together with the corn kernels. Season carefully—there should be enough cayenne pepper to give it warmth, but not overpower—and pour the mixture into the tart shell. Bake for 25–30 minutes until golden, puffed up, and just set. Let cool for 10 minutes before serving, accompanied by peppery watercress or landcress with garlicky dressing.

HOMITY PIES

I remember eating homity pies years ago in the original Cranks restaurant in Marshall Street, London, just behind Carnaby Street. I first attempted my own version of them—without the mushrooms which I remember in the original—when my two oldest children were tiny. I really favor a whole wheat crust here, but it is entirely up to you. They are brilliant picnic food: substantial and not prone to disintegrate in the lap. We take them well wrapped in tinfoil on the way to Ireland, and they still have that lovely memory of warmth about them even after hours in the car.

Serves 6

pie dough made with 1½ cups
flour (page 139), chilled
¾ lb peeled potatoes
2 tbsp butter
3–4 tbsp milk or cream
1 lb onions, finely chopped
3 tbsp olive oil
2 garlic cloves, crushed
2 tbsp chopped fresh flat-
leaf parsley, or mixed
parsley, chives, and thyme
1 cup mature Cheddar,
grated
salt and pepper
2 ripe tomatoes, thinly sliced

Roll out the dough thinly and use it to line six individual greased tart pans, 4 inches in diameter. If you don't have individual tart pans, make one large tart in a 12-inch pan. Preheat the oven to 425°F. Bake the tart shell blind for 10 minutes in the smaller pans, 15 in the large one. Remove the beans and return the tart shell to the oven for 5 minutes.

Boil the potatoes until cooked, drain, then mash them with the butter and milk or cream. Sauté the onions in the oil until golden and softened. Stir into the potato mixture with the garlic, herbs, half the cheese, and the seasoning. Let cool to at least tepid.

Fill the tart shells with the mixture, sprinkle with the remaining cheese, place a slice of tomato on top, and bake in the oven for 20 minutes, until gratinéed and goldenly bubbling on top. Let cool slightly before eating or wrapping in tinfoil for a picnic.

Breakfast Tart

This started off as a joke, but then it got serious. Having declared authoritatively that there wasn't an occasion or time of day at which a tart wouldn't please and delight, I got to thinking about breakfast. Serious breakfast. The full-monty sort of English breakfast: eggs, bacon, blood pudding, broiled tomatoes. The accompanying toast is, like pasta, the vehicle on which the rich, succulently flavored proteins travel best, so why not encase the whole thing in pastry instead? The result was glorious, a great brunch, or lunch or supper if you think it's a p.m. sort of a tart.

The secret is not to turn it into a mobile junkyard, and not to overstuff it, or the individual flavors lose out. Mushrooms, I feel, are a flavor too far, but you might prefer them if you are not a blood pudding convert like me. My inspiration was dotting it with cherry tomatoes rolled in olive oil and warmed in the oven first. They burst on the tongue with flavor, and cut a dash through all the rich, eggy, meaty protein.

Serves 6

9-inch unbaked tart shell, chilled (page 139)

2–3 strips of oak-smoked organic bacon

3 slices of blood pudding or ½ lb cleaned mushrooms

a pat of butter

12–15 organic cherry tomatoes

a splash of olive oil

1 egg and 2 egg yolks (I used duck eggs)

1 cup organic heavy cream

3 tbsp whole milk (optional, see method)

pepper

Preheat the oven to 400°F. Bake the tart shell blind for 10 minutes, then remove the beans, prick the bottom with a fork, brush with beaten egg, and return to the oven for 5 minutes. Remove from the oven and turn the heat down to 350°F. Meanwhile, prepare the filling.

Snip the bacon into pieces and cook without additional fat in a small skillet until crisply frizzled. Drain on paper towels. Fry your blood pudding in butter until browned on both sides or fry the mushrooms until tender. Drain. Cut the blood pudding slices into quarters. Put the tomatoes in a heatproof bowl and pour about ½ tablespoon of olive oil over them. Shake to coat, and put them in the oven for 10 minutes.

Whip your eggs and cream—and milk if you're using it—together and season with pepper. I thinned my custard down with milk since I was using richer eggs; the duck eggs turned the tart a heavenly golden color.

Scatter the blood pudding (or mushrooms) and bacon over the tart shell, then add your tomatoes strategically, and gently place the tart on a baking sheet on the oven rack. Pour in the custard carefully from a pitcher, and slide the baking sheet into the oven. Cook for about 35 minutes, let cool for 10 minutes, then invert, and serve.

"*It is difficult to meet an ungenerous cook. The very heart of the experience of making food is about sharing, nurture, generosity, the giving of pleasure.*"

OTHER PEOPLE'S TARTS

Richard Corrigan's Banana Tart (page 78)

Broccoli, Blue Cheese, and Crème Fraîche Tart

In Britain, no one has done as much as Nigel Slater in the way of making people just want to cook, and in inspiring the confidence to do so. He is one of Britain's most respected young food writers. His columns are rich, delicious, and, like all the best food, wickedly sexy. His writing is totally seductive.

I went to interview him for Food Illustrated, *and spent a blissful few hours talking to him about his childhood, his career, and the writing that evokes in his readers the pleasure and comfort of knowing that he's really just one of them, simply hungering after a good dinner. "I want people to relax and stop thinking they've got to put on a show. The nicest things are the simplest." I think his heart is really in baking, which he began to learn about after his mother's death when he was a boy of nine. The afternoon I spent with him, he'd made scones, and the most delicious, crumbly, buttery, lavender biscuits, with the sort of taste you want to bottle. Try this tart of his; it is perfect as a light lunch or supper.*

Serves 6–8

⅓ lb broccoli, ideally purple
    sprouting
3 tbsp olive oil
1 medium onion, finely sliced
a few sprigs of fresh thyme
4 garlic cloves, peeled
4 anchovy fillets, chopped
¾ cup pungent blue cheese
    such as Gorgonzola or
    Fourme d'Ambert
1 tsp capers, rinsed
1 cup crème fraîche
pepper
13 oz (by weight) puff pastry
    (chilled ready-rolled
    is fine here)
Parmesan for grating

Preheat the oven to 425°F.

Rinse the broccoli thoroughly and drop it into boiling, salted water. Let it cook until tender—about 7 minutes, depending on the type. Drain, pat dry on paper towels, and set aside. Return the empty saucepan to the heat and add the olive oil, onion, thyme, and the whole garlic cloves. Let them stew to softness over moderate heat. They should be golden and tender after 10 minutes or so.

Chop the drained broccoli roughly and add it to the onions with the chopped anchovies, crumbled cheese, capers, and crème fraîche. Grind in a little pepper and then let the mixture cool.

Open up the dough, or roll your own into a 14 x 9-inch rectangle, and place it on a lightly floured baking sheet. Score a line, without going right through the dough, along each side, about 1 inch from the edge. Spread the broccoli mixture over the center of the dough, taking it as far as the line you have scored, and leaving a clear border. This will rise and form a rim during cooking. Scatter with grated Parmesan.

Bake in the preheated oven for 15–20 minutes. Check after 15; it will cook very quickly. You want the edges to be dark golden brown and crisp. Serve at once, with salad on the side.

George Morley's Leek Tart

I first met George (Georgina) when my agent George (Georgina) was perambulating me around the publishers trying to sell my book Last Letters Home. *I remember saying to agent George "she is the only one I really want to work with." It was obvious that George really wanted to do the book, she doesn't hide her enthusiasm under a bushel, and there is nothing more confidence-inspiring to the doubtful writer than the enthusiasm and belief of a good editor. Thus began an extremely happy partnership, which nowadays is confined to greedy weekends rather than work.*

There is no one I am happier working with in a kitchen. George is obsessively knowledgeable, and equally as greedy as me, and when she comes to stay with her husband, Shawn, and young son, Charlie, we plan the food in slavering telephone calls. I'd like to think we inspire each other to greater heights of culinary achievement. Not that we aim for kitchen pyrotechnics, but we do like to bask in cooking the unknown, untested delight for each other, a discreet bit of one-upmanship, or, if people are coming, perform an extraordinarily harmonious double act in the small space that is my kitchen. I know that if she says "What about a caramelized apple pavlova?" she will get stuck in and do it, and it will be sublime.

Serves 6—8
3 lbs leeks
large pat of butter
 (about ½ cup!)
1 cup sour cream
2 eggs, beaten
salt, pepper, and paprika

Cheese pastry
¾ cup strong Cheddar,
 grated
6 tbsp butter
2 cups flour
pinch of salt
ice water to blend

For the cheese pastry dough (which is basically Arabella Boxer's recipe for cheese dough), process the cheese and butter into the flour with the salt. Add ice water slowly until the mixture comes together. Let rest in the refrigerator for at least an hour before rolling out and lining a 10-inch tart pan. Preheat the oven to 400°F. Brush the tart shell with a little beaten egg and bake blind (no need for baking beans) for 15—20 minutes. Turn the oven down to 350°F.

Slice the leeks and rinse if gritty. Discard any really tough dark green bits. Sauté in a very generous pat of butter until completely softened, but do not let them brown. Let cool slightly.

Mix the sour cream with the beaten eggs and add the leeks. Season with salt and pepper and shake in enough paprika to turn the mixture a very pale rusty pink—about ½ teaspoon should do it. Pour into the tart shell and bake for about 20 minutes, or until just set. It should be wobbly in the middle. Best served about 15 minutes after it emerges from the oven, when it is still warm but not piping hot.

Cousin Deborah's Cheese Strata

Deborah and I are first cousins and have enjoyed food together since our childhood Sunday lunches with our mutual grandparents in Sussex. Their cook, Rhoda, would usually have a gargantuan sirloin or baron of beef brought to the table, often with a turkey in case that's what the grandchildren preferred, and at least six vegetables from the amazing kitchen garden. And then there were the nursery desserts: cloud-topped lemon meringue pies, Bakewell tarts, ice creams, treacle tarts, steamed chocolate puddings, lemon mousses, with pitchers of thick ivory cream from the farm. We still talk about those lunches, and have kept on the tradition for our children, who all appreciate good food, and thank God like one another independently of the fact that they happen to be cousins. Deborah is an exceptionally fine cook, wonderful to work with in the kitchen, and I don't believe we've ever quarreled in or out of it, a miracle in the midst of family fallouts. When she brought her boys, Alexander and Oliver, out to Ireland last summer, we cooked frenziedly for five days, relishing the chatter, the greed, and the absence of pressure when two equals equal half the work.

The absence of dough would, strictly, disqualify this dish from inclusion in this book, but in every other aspect it meets my demands of a fine savory tart: cheesy, eggy, creamy, self-contained, and great to serve after the theater or a movie, with salad. It is refrigerated for 24 hours before cooking, so plan ahead.

Serves 6 but can be stretched

4 strips thinly sliced bacon

1 tsp olive oil

1 medium onion, chopped very small

about 6 tbsp butter, softened

5 slices of good-quality one-day-old bread

1½ cups mature Cheddar, grated

4 eggs, beaten lightly

2 cups light cream

¼ tsp paprika

¼ tsp chili powder

1 tsp mustard powder

Sauté the bacon in the oil until crisp, drain it on paper towels, and chop it into small pieces. Sauté the onion in the same pan until soft, but not colored, then remove with a slotted spoon.

Butter the bread on one side, and cut into cubes. Line an 11-inch flan dish with half the bread cubes. Sprinkle with half the cheese. Put the rest of the bread into the flan dish and scatter over the rest of the cheese. Whip together the eggs, cream, and spices, and pour them over the top. Refrigerate for 24 hours.

Preheat the oven to 350°F. Bake the strata for an hour and let stand for 5–10 minutes before serving.

This is also delicious with lightly poached haddock between the layers of bread, and sautéed mushrooms rather than bacon.

SLOW-ROASTED TOMATO TART

I bumped into Celia Brooks Brown in my favorite cookbook shop. Books for Cooks, in Blenheim Crescent in Notting Hill, makes the amateur, the ingenue, the serious and the professional cook feel at home. There is always someone knowledgeable to give advice, help with a query, trace a difficult-to-find tome, or put one on to something utterly new and inspiring. I spend whole mornings there, infrequently, but they are invaluable for research, inspiration, ideas, and for making one realize how frighteningly much more there is to learn. There is a little café at the back, where cooks come in on a rota basis and make lunch. If you can get a table, you are likely to be fed by a fledgling or fully fledged cook, say, trying out recipes for a new book. This morning, Celia was making a Black Forest meringue, with cherries on stalks sunken glossily into the cream. We got to talking, and I ended up buying her book Vegetarian Foodscape, *from which this recipe comes.*

Serves 6

9-inch unbaked tart shell,
　chilled (page 139)

3 lbs ripe plum tomatoes

6 garlic cloves,
　sliced wafer thin

4 tbsp olive oil

2 tbsp balsamic vinegar

salt and pepper

a little sugar

3 egg yolks (and 1 white for
　brushing the tart bottom)

⅔ cup crème fraîche

2 handfuls of basil leaves

Preheat the oven to 375°F. Bake the tart shell blind for 15 minutes, then remove the beans, and return to the oven for 5 minutes. Brush egg white over the tart shell, and let cool. Turn the heat down to 300°F.

Place the tomatoes in a bowl and pour boiling water over them. Spike each one with the point of a knife, and drain after 1 minute. Pour cold water over them and drain it off immediately; they will now be cool enough to handle. Slip them out of their skins, slice them in half vertically, and place them cut side up in a roasting dish. Lay the garlic slices inside the tomato halves. Dribble the olive oil and balsamic vinegar into the halves and sprinkle with salt, pepper, and a little sugar. Roast in the oven for about 1 hour, until shrunken and brown around the edges.

Arrange the roasted tomatoes in the tart shell, adding any juices from the roasting dish. Mix together the egg yolks and crème fraîche, and tear in the basil leaves. Season with salt and pepper, and pour the mixture over the tomatoes. Bake for 30–40 minutes, until the custard is set and lightly browned. Let it stand for 10 minutes before inverting and serving.

TOMATO TARTE TATIN

Lindsey Bareham's The Big Red Book of Tomatoes *is a compendium of wonderful tomato recipes gathered from around the world, or all the countries where the tomato is as staple an ingredient as the potato, which she has also written a definitive book about. What I like about her unpretentious writing is how she elevates humble ingredients thriftily, imaginatively, into the most delicious recipes. She would always use the best olive oil, the best ham, but every extravagance is carefully considered within the context of creating wonderful food reasonably. We met when I went to interview her about the book, having not seen each other for 25 years, since I briefly went out with her brother.*

Serves 4

1 heaping tsp sugar

salt and black pepper

1 tbsp balsamic vinegar

4 tbsp olive oil

1¾ lbs medium tomatoes, peeled, cored, and halved through the core

5 oz puff pastry (page 141)

To serve

¼ cup Parmesan

a few basil leaves

Preheat the oven to 400°F. Lightly oil a 7-inch tart pan.

Dissolve the sugar and a little salt and pepper in the vinegar, then whisk in 3 tablespoons of the oil. Place the tomato halves, rounded sides down, in the pan, nudging them close together so that they are slightly on their sides. Pour the dressing over the top.

On a floured surface, roll the dough quite thinly and lay over the top of the pan. Cut around the edge, and lightly tuck the dough down the sides like a blanket. Brush the remaining olive oil over the top of the dough. Place in the oven and cook for about 20 minutes, until the crust is puffed and scorched.

Remove from the oven and run a knife around the edge of the shell. Carefully drain most of the liquid into a small pitcher. Place a large plate over the tart and quickly invert. Set aside to cool slightly.

To serve, whip the dressing and pour it over the tomatoes. Grate over the Parmesan, snip over the basil, and slice the tart into four wedges. This is very good eaten with peas mixed with pesto that has been slackened with a little olive oil.

Cherry Tomato Tarte Tatin

Serves 4

7 oz (by weight) puff pastry
4 tbsp extra virgin olive oil
1¼ lbs organic cherry
   tomatoes, stalks removed
8 tbsp balsamic vinegar
port or Madeira (optional)
salt and freshly ground black
   pepper

Preheat the oven to 425°F. Divide the puff pastry into four and roll into very thin 5-inch discs, or one large disc. Pour 1 tablespoon of the oil into each of four 4-inch tart pans, or into an 8-inch tart pan, swirl it around, then arrange the whole tomatoes in a single layer.

Heat the balsamic vinegar in a small saucepan and reduce until sticky and caramelized, adding a splash of port or Madeira if you have it on hand. Season the tomatoes with salt and pepper, then pour over a dribble of the vinegar. Cover with a puff pastry disc, tucking the pastry into the pans. Bake for 8 – 10 minutes, until the pastry is puffed and golden. Check assiduously; a larger tart will take longer.

Remove from the oven, run a knife around the edge of the pastry, then place a plate over each tart and quickly invert. *Note*! There could be quite a lot of liquid surrounding the tarts.

Blue Cheese Tart
with Red Onion Marmalade

I can't remember when I first went to Markwick's, Judy and Stephen Markwick's wonderful restaurant in Bristol, but I have never had a bad meal there, and if you think that sounds like faint praise, I have only ever eaten exceptionally well there over the years. Stephen's set lunch used to be the best value I know; now that I no longer work in Bristol, I only ever go to dinner there. He is, quite simply, a very good cook. Stephen is in the kitchen, not dancing table attendance or on television. Judy is out there talking to the customers, and gently but knowledgeably steering them through the wine list and the menu.

Serves 6
¼ cup mascarpone
¼ cup heavy cream
3 egg yolks
1½ cups blue cheese,
  crumbled (a mixture
  of Roquefort, Stilton, and
  Shropshire Blue)
wilted spinach (optional)
salt, pepper, and a pinch
  of cayenne pepper

Red onion marmalade
2 red onions, thinly sliced
pinch of salt, pepper,
  and sugar
4 tbsp butter
2 tbsp sherry vinegar
4 tbsp red wine

Preheat the oven to 375°F. Line six individual tart pans with either puff pastry (see page 141) or pie dough (page 139) made with 1 cup flour, and bake blind. Remove from the oven and turn the heat up to 425°F.

Make the red onion marmalade by mixing the onions in a bowl with salt, pepper, and sugar. Heat the butter in a saucepan until foamy and add the onions, stirring well. When almost cooked down, add the vinegar and red wine, and simmer gently until well reduced.

Make the tart filling by beating together the mascarpone, cream, and egg yolks until smooth, then stir in the blue cheese and seasoning. Place a spoonful of the onion marmalade in the bottom of each tart shell (you can also add wilted spinach leaves if you like) and then fill each one with the blue cheese mixture, and bake in a hot oven for approximately 10–15 minutes. Good served with chutney, something like green tomato.

Sutlu Börek
Creamy Cheese Bake with Filo Pastry

This is not strictly a tart, but recently I went to the launch of Claudia Roden's book Tamarind and Spice, *where she cooked so many wonderful dishes I decided I couldn't leave her out of this book. I think her influence has been profound, starting with her original* Book of Middle Eastern Food *back in 1968. Nobody, she told me, wrote down recipes in Egypt when she was a girl there, everything was passed down from grandmother and mother to daughter. Claudia didn't even realize that her family ate Jewish Egyptian food until she left to come to London as an art student. She is both food writer and cultural historian, whose record of the traditional food and cooking of the Jewish people is a work of extraordinary scholarship and dedication, both fascinating and accessible, as is all her food writing. This is a Turkish recipe, with leaves of filo pastry baked with a light, creamy custard.*

Serves 4

1¼ cups feta cheese
1¼ cups cottage cheese
4 large eggs
3 tbsp chopped flat-leaf parsley
5 sheets filo pastry
2 tbsp unsalted butter, melted
2 cups milk

Preheat the oven to 350°F.

To prepare the filling, mash the feta with a fork and mix with the cottage cheese, 1 egg, and the parsley.

Open out the sheets of filo, leaving them in a pile. Brush the top one lightly with melted butter and then fit it, buttered side up, into an oiled round baking dish about 12 inches in diameter, leaving it overhanging at the sides. Fit the second sheet over it and brush lightly with butter. Spread the filling evenly over the pastry. Cover with the remaining sheets of filo, brushing each with melted butter, and finally folding them over the mixture. Fold the top one so that it presents a smooth surface and brush with butter. Bake for 15 minutes until lightly colored, then remove from the oven.

Lightly beat the remaining 3 eggs with the milk and pour over the hot pie; you do not need to add salt as the feta is very salty. Return to the oven and bake for about 30 minutes or until the custard is absorbed and set and the top of the pastry is golden. Serve hot, cut into wedges.

FEUILLÉTÉ AUX POIRES

This is the tart, if such a word is up to describing this stratospherically brilliant creation, that changed my teenage perception of food overnight. It is, retrospectively, something that has had an extraordinary influence on my cooking life, showing me, as it did, a level of cooking that went beyond anything I had suspected possible, yet remaining trenchantly rooted in the real world of achievable, good honest cooking.

When I first wrote to Pierre Koffmann's office to ask if I could have the recipe, I was informed that I certainly could, but as he was in transit between restaurants and homes, I would have to wait. Several months and several calls later, I decided on a more direct approach, and rang my culinary hero at The Berkeley. He rang me back, and charmingly explained what to do, all of 25 years after I had first tasted it! I think reinterpreting Monsieur Koffmann's description would be sacrilegious, so am breaking with tradition and reproducing the conversation we had as faithfully as possible. How you poach your pear and make your caramel I leave to you. My pear goes into a vanilla sugared syrupy bath with a touch of lemon, and is poached until cooked.

"Cut the puff pastry out around the shape of the pear, and cook it until it is just done. Then, with the tip of a knife, cut around the bottom of the pastry, and remove the inside, leaving the bottom layer. Return to the oven for 3–5 minutes to dry out. Fill the tart shell with crème légère when it is cool—crème patissiere with the same amount of whipped cream added to it—then put your poached pear half on top."

"I seem to remember a sabayon with some eau de vie de poires?"

"Well, you wouldn't put that over the top because of the texture of the caramel [a thin layer of which he covers the pear with], but you might put it underneath, or you could add a drop of Poires Williams to the crème légère instead. If you have any problem, please ring again."

And with that he was gone.

Thank you, Monsieur Koffmann. In your quiet, unshowy way you have set the standard in London for two decades, and never resorted to the brash celebrity chef publicity stunts that so many have. We know that you are still in your kitchen, and that your food is as suffused with brilliance as it is with honesty.

MEYER LEMON TARTS

I met the inimitable Jeffrey Steingarten in New York last October, and attempted to interview him for Food Illustrated. *Jeffrey doesn't answer questions, like all good lawyers, he just tells you what he wants to tell you. Before he became* Vogue's *food critic, and wrote the wonderful* The Man Who Ate Everything, *he was indeed a Harvard lawyer. Small detail is, alongside food, the staff of Jeffrey's life, and he told me the following:"Frank Meyer introduced the eponymous lemon to America in 1905. He was an agricultural adventurist who'd found one growing in a pot in Peking. They are like Sicilian lemons, sweeter, less acid, and more full of flavor than most lemons. They don't grow on the East Coast of America, but I grow them in San Diego."*

Makes 6 individual tarts
¾ cup cold unsalted butter
1 large egg yolk
½ cup confectioners' sugar
1 tbsp and a bit of heavy
    cream
2 cups unbleached flour

Meyer lemon cream filling
4 Meyer lemons
1 cup vanilla sugar
4 large eggs
¾ cup cold heavy cream

Make the dough in a food processor: blend the butter, egg yolk, confectioners' sugar, and cream until smooth (about 30 seconds), scraping down halfway through and at the end. Add the flour and blend just until the dough becomes a ball, about 5 seconds. Break into six pieces, flatten them, wrap, and refrigerate for an hour.

On a floured surface, roll each piece out to a rough circle about 6 inches across and ⅛-inch thick. Prick holes with a fork all over the dough. With a palette knife or spatula, lift a circle of dough and drape it over an individual tart pan, 4 inches in diameter and ⅞-inch high. Gently coax the dough down into the ring without stretching it. Now, rotating the ring as you go, push straight down along its sides so that the dough closely lines the bottom and sides. Do the same with five more rings. Set them on a baking sheet lined with brown paper. Freeze for at least 30 minutes before baking.

Preheat the oven to 375°F. Bake the pastry for 15–18 minutes, until golden. With a spatula, transfer the pastry shells to a wire rack, and remove the rings with tongs.

For the filling, lightly grate the yellow skin of three of the lemons. Squeeze the juice of all four. Put the sugar and lemon zest in a saucepan. Whisk in the eggs and lemon juice. Heat gently, stirring constantly with a whisk, until the mixture thickens and pales. Immediately strain the mixture through a strainer into a bowl. Let it cool to room temperature, stirring occasionally. Whip the cream until stiff, and fold it into the cooled custard. Spoon the mixture into the pastry shells.

CHERRY AND ALMOND TART

I was alerted to this tart through Simon Hopkinson's column in The Independent *newspaper, on a week when he was writing about "absolute and cherished favorites." That was enough for me. Simon is one of the select band of food writers who has had a huge influence on my food over the years, and who actually writes in a way that impels one to cook the recipe just as soon as one can lay one's hands on the ingredients. He is the kind of person who I know I would enjoy sitting down to a good dinner with; his passion for food is infectious.*

This tart is one he poached from Malcolm Reid and Colin Long, erstwhile proprietors of the famous Box Tree at Ilkley in Yorkshire, that I, like Simon, unfortunately never ate at. He describes this recipe of theirs as "one of their most simple and impeccable." He is right.

Serves 6–8

1 cup all-purpose flour
4 tbsp butter, cut into cubes
pinch of salt
1 egg yolk
1–2 tbsp ice water
a little beaten egg
2 rounded tbsp apricot jam

For the filling

½ cup unsalted butter, softened
½ cup sugar, plus extra for serving
2 large eggs
1 cup ground almonds
grated zest of 1 lemon
2½ cups (drained weight) pitted, bottled morello cherries

In a food processor, blend together the flour, butter, and salt, then tip them into a large bowl and gently mix in the egg yolk and water with cool hands or a knife, until well amalgamated. Chill in the refrigerator for at least an hour.

Preheat the oven to 375°F. Line a 9-inch tart pan with the dough and bake blind for 15–20 minutes. Remove the beans, brush the tart shell with beaten egg, and return to the oven for a further 10 minutes, until it is golden, crisp, and well cooked, particularly the bottom. Warm the jam slightly and spoon over the bottom of the tart. Let cool. Turn the oven down to 350°F.

For the filling, beat together the butter and sugar until light and fluffy. Add 1 egg and continue beating until entirely incorporated, then add the other egg and beat again. Add the ground almonds and lemon zest and fold them in thoroughly. Spoon into the tart shell and smooth the top. Press the cherries into the mixture, pushing them under the almond paste with your fingers.

Return to the oven and bake for 40 minutes or so, until the surface is golden brown, puffed up, and springy to the touch. Switch off the oven and leave the tart there with the door ajar for 15 minutes. Dust with sugar before serving.

APRICOT FRANGIPANE TART

In an ideal world, I'd live so close to Baker and Spice in Walton Street, London, that I could smell the yeasty baking smells all day. They are quite simply the best baker and patissier I know this side of the English Channel. No croissants get near theirs; flaky, buttery, with an almost sandy, grainy texture, light yet substantial, with that wonderful stretchy, Lycra-ey core that resists being pulled apart, but is golden and soft when you get to it. Dan Lepard, their bread guru, asked me to mention "something sweet about Gail Stephens [the shop's founder and owner]. It is a very special bakery and we are proud of what we have created." I am gradually working my way through their tarts, cakes, and the traiteur department, and this is the recipe Dan developed at Alastair Little's restaurant, after a story told him by a French patissier. "The pit of a soft fruit contains not just the heart of the flavor, but also the knowledge of the plant that bore it. It is essential to use a stone when cooking any fruit. Possibly a romantic notion, but I believed it." The apricots stand proud in this tart, with beautifully singed tips.

Serves 8

16 firm blush apricots

7 oz (by weight) rich puff
   pastry

½ cup soft set apricot
   preserve

Frangipane

2 cups ground almonds,
   plus the kernels from
   3 of the apricots

⅔ cup sugar

1 cup unsalted butter,
   softened

3 organic eggs

⅞ cup all-purpose flour

Preheat the oven to 350°F. Halve the apricots with a small, sharp knife, and remove the pits. Crack three of the pits with a hammer to extract the kernels.

For the frangipane, place the almonds, apricot kernels, and sugar in a food processor and process until the kernels have blended with the sugar and almonds. Next add the butter and mix until pale and smooth. Beat in the eggs, one by one, then finally lightly beat in the flour. Transfer the mixture to a small container and leave in a cool place while preparing the dough.

Roll out the dough into a thin circle large enough to cover and overlap the sides of a 10-inch tart ring. Place the ring on a baking sheet lined with wax paper. Gently press the dough down into the ring, and prick the bottom of the pastry lightly with a fork. Put the shell in the refrigerator to chill for 10–15 minutes.

Spread the frangipane over the bottom of the tart, then sit the apricot halves upright in the frangipane. Place the tart in the center of the oven and bake for 15 minutes. Reduce the heat to 325°F and continue baking for 35–45 minutes, until the crust is crisp and the frangipane light brown in color. Warm the apricot preserve in a saucepan over low heat, with a little water to make a syrup, and brush this over the tart. Invert and serve warm with crème fraîche.

CHOCOLATE AND APRICOT TART

It was September last year when Neale Whitaker sent me to Jerez to write about sherry for Food Illustrated with Mark Sainsbury and chef Sam Clark, two of the co-owners of Moro. We had an amazing four days, and an even more amazing four nights, culminating in the all-night flamenco in the Buleria to celebrate the grape harvest. We worshipped at the shrine that Sam and Mark had wanted to visit, the bodega of Miguel Valdespino, one of the last of the family-run sherry-making businesses, and spent hours drinking his sherries and appraising his sherry vinegars. We also ate seafood like I have never eaten, from at least nine kinds of prawns to unknown delights like "ventresca"—belly of tuna—and sea anemones that we'd seen arrive minutes before in a fisherman's boat. A nine-course dinner at Miguel's brother's restaurant, La Mesa Rodonda, combined the strong flavors of southern Spain with the delicate spicing of North Africa. On our return, we vowed to have a reunion, so we met up at Moro in Clerkenwell, London. We followed delicious tapas and Valdespino sherry with briks of crab, and partridge, and then I couldn't resist their chocolate and apricot tart. They make it with a dense, tart apricot paste which is sold in Iranian shops in long, flat strips. If you can't find this, use apricot jam instead, with a little lemon juice. It is important that the apricot layer is slightly tart so that it cuts through the rich chocolate.

Serves 8–10

2 cups all-purpose flour
⅔ cup confectioners' sugar
⅔ cup unsalted butter
2 egg yolks

For the filling

½ cup apricot paste,
   or apricot jam mixed with
   the juice of
   ½ a lemon
¾ cup unsalted butter
7 oz (7 squares) bittersweet
   chocolate
4 eggs
1 cup sugar

Make the dough in a food processor: combine the flour, confectioners' sugar, and butter until evenly blended. Add the egg yolks and continue to blend until the ingredients come together. Wrap in plastic wrap and refrigerate for half an hour. Preheat the oven to 400°F. Roll out the dough and line a 12-inch tart pan. Bake blind for 15 minutes, then remove the beans, prick the bottom with a fork, and return to the oven for 5 minutes.

To make the filling: if you are using apricot paste, melt it in a saucepan with a little water, then spread it over the bottom of the tart. Alternatively, spread over a thin layer of the apricot jam. Melt the butter and chocolate together in a double boiler. Whisk the eggs and sugar together until they are pale and light. Gently fold the chocolate mixture into the eggs and sugar. Transfer to the tart shell, and even out with the back of a spoon. Turn the oven down to 350°F and bake the tart for 20 minutes, or until the chocolate has formed a slight crust. Let cool slightly, then invert, and serve with yogurt or crème fraîche.

SIMON HOPKINSON'S CHOCOLATE TART

If there is a heaven, this is it. I speak as a hopeless chocoholic, not that I am remotely interested in weaning myself off the stuff. We had briefly corresponded, and Simon had kindly agreed to my using any of his recipes I wanted to; this one is from his book Roast Chicken and Other Stories, *which I go back to time and time again, not that I ever leave it for very long in between whiles. After all, there are things in it like this chocolate tart, which rates as one of the mega culinary experiences of all time.*

If anyone is insane enough to believe they can do better, I want to hear about it. The only tinkering I have ever done is to make a cocoa dough with Green and Black's organic cocoa, but the original way is unparalleled.

Serves 8
¾ cup butter
⅔ cup confectioners' sugar
2 egg yolks
2 cups all-purpose flour

For the filling
2 eggs
3 egg yolks
5 tbsp sugar
⅔ cup unsalted butter
7 oz (7 squares) best bitter
   chocolate, broken
   into pieces

To make the dough, put the butter, confectioners' sugar, and egg yolks in a bowl or food processor and work together quickly. Blend in the flour, and work to a homogeneous paste. Chill for at least 1 hour.

Preheat the oven to 350°F. Roll out the dough as thinly as you can, and line a 10-inch tart pan. Bake blind for about 25 minutes, or until pale biscuit-colored, but thoroughly cooked through. Remove from the oven and increase the temperature to 375°F.

To make the filling, put the eggs, yolks, and sugar in a bowl and beat vigorously together, preferably with an electric mixer, until really thick and fluffy. Melt the butter and chocolate together in a bowl over a saucepan of barely simmering water, stirring until smooth. Pour onto the egg mixture while just warm. Briefly beat together until well amalgamated, then pour into the tart shell. Return to the hot oven for 5 minutes, then remove and let cool. Serve with heavy cream.

SALLY CLARKE'S PRUNE TART

I have always admired Sally Clarke's food. Dinner at her eponymous Kensington Church Street restaurant is one menu, with no choice, unless you happen not to like one of the dishes. You have to be very good to get away with it, and she is. So often I have languished over long menus, utterly unable to make a decision, just wanting someone else to. If you go to her restaurant you have already taken away the burden of choice; it is like going to a friend's for dinner and speculating excitedly on what she's cooked. In her next-door shop there is a café, breads, cakes, cheeses, vegetables, and cream of the absolute best, and her chocolate truffles, which are the last word in temptation.

The other day I was having lunch in the café with a friend; I had a divine slice of chocolate cake, but his prune tart was diviner. I came home and faxed Sally for the recipe, and here it is.

Serves 8
½ cup butter
½ cup confectioners' sugar
2 small egg yolks
1½ cups all-purpose flour

For the filling
12 pitted prunes
a little tea, cognac,
    and orange juice
1 egg and 2 yolks
6 tbsp sugar
1 tsp pure vanilla extract,
    or the scraped–out
    contents of 1 vanilla bean
1¼ cups heavy cream
⅓ cup milk

Soak the prunes overnight in a splash each of tea, cognac, and orange juice.

To make the dough, put the butter, confectioners' sugar, and egg yolks in a bowl or food processor and work together quickly. Blend in the flour, and work to a homogeneous paste. Chill for at least 1 hour.

Preheat the oven to 350°F. Roll out the dough thinly and line a 9-inch tart pan. Bake blind for about 25 minutes, or until crisp and golden. Remove from the oven and turn the heat down to 300°F.

Beat the egg and yolks with the sugar and vanilla until smooth. Heat the cream and milk together until hot, and pour over the egg mixture. Strain and leave on one side to cool slightly.

Place the prunes in the tart shell and pour the custard over the prunes. Bake for 20 – 25 minutes or until lightly set. Serve cool, with whipped cream.

Fig Tarts

There is nowhere I would rather eat, no chef I would more happily converse with, or spend a day in the kitchen with, than the talented Irishman Richard Corrigan of Lindsay House. The restaurant dining room is unfashionably intimate and linen laden; the location, a creakily corridored Georgian town house in Soho. Down in the bowels of the kitchen, Richard practises the ancient arts of curing, potting, and brining. No bit of meat escapes him, from snout to tail, and all his produce comes from impeccable sources, be it smoked eel or the freshest of Dover soles cooked with brown shrimps and cucumber. The hospitality at Lindsay House could only be Irish: relaxed, warm, effortless, full of generosity. I'll wager a tart his Michelin star will be doubled.

Makes 6 individual tarts
8oz (by weight) puff pastry
6–8 ripe figs
2 tbsp unsalted butter, melted

Frangipane
2 tbsp sugar
2 tbsp ground almonds
½ tsp cornflour
2 tbsp unsalted butter

Preheat the oven to 400°F. Roll out the pastry and stamp out six 4-inch circles; place the circles on a lightly greased baking sheet.

Make the frangipane by mixing all the ingredients together until smooth. Spread a little of the mixture on to each pastry circle. Thinly slice the figs and arrange in a circular fashion on top of the frangipane. Brush the tops with melted butter and bake for 12–15 minutes. Serve warm or cool.

Banana Tart

Another fantastic recipe from the talented Richard Corrigan. He serves this tart with raisin syrup and rum cream. I suggest some cold crème anglaise or a little snifter of dark rum and brown sugar beaten into some good heavy cream.

Serves 8

just over 1 lb puff pastry
   (page 141)
8 ripe but firm small
   bananas
a pat of unsalted butter,
   melted
confectioners' sugar

Frangipane

½ cup unsalted butter,
   softened
½ cup sugar
1 egg and 1 yolk
1 cup ground almonds
3 tbsp all-purpose flour

Roll out the dough and stamp out eight 4-inch squares or 5-inch discs. Place them on a baking sheet lined with brown paper. With the back of a knife blade, draw a rim just inside each disc, and prick the center with a fork. Chill in the refrigerator for at least 30 minutes. Preheat the oven to 400°F.

For the frangipane, cream the butter and sugar in an electric mixer until pale and fluffy. Add the beaten egg and yolk, then the almonds and flour, beating all the while. Spoon the mixture into the middle of each pastry disc, leaving the rim clear, and enough space for a band of sliced bananas to surround the frangipane. Fan the bananas around, closely overlapping, then top the frangipane with the remaining slices. Brush with melted butter, then finish with a fine dusting of sifted sugar. Bake for about 20 minutes, until the bananas are caramelized and shiny and the pastry puffed up and golden. Domestic ovens are not always good at caramelizing, but you can always brûlée the banana tops with a bit more confectioners' sugar and a blowtorch when they come out of the oven. Serve hot.

RHUBARB MERINGUE PIE

When Nigella Lawson's book How to Eat, The Pleasures and Principles of Good Food *came out, a lot of serious cookbook junkies, myself very much included, breathed a sigh of relief. The preponderance of celebrity chef's books, with restaurant recipes, had left us feeling inadequate, exhausted, hungry for sheer simplicity, but the best. And not just for another "How To" manual. Some of us are also looking for brilliant writing and a distinctive style, not a professional's dishes ghosted into a prose style that is clearly not the author's voice. Well, Nigella's had it all. She also gave credit for all the recipes she'd snitched from others. Where things come from I find fascinating, as fascinating as what they've been transmuted into.*

We met when I went to interview her for Food Illustrated, *and became friends as a result. And as "allies", Nigella wrote when inscribing my copy of her book. This is the recipe she wanted me to include, which she dedicates, in her book, to her sister Horatia. It is utterly delicious, and not just as a tart. I have lots of rhubarb left when I've cooked it for jam, so I make rhubarb meringue pudding out of the top two-thirds of this recipe, omitting the pastry.*

Serves 6

just under 2 lbs rhubarb,
  untrimmed weight
juice of ½ an orange
2 eggs, separated
⅔ cup plus ½ cup sugar
2 tbsp all-purpose flour
2 tbsp unsalted butter,
  melted
¼ tsp cream of tartar

Make pie dough (page 139) with 1 cup flour, using orange juice instead of water to make it cohere. Chill, then line a 9-inch tart pan. Preheat the oven to 400°F. Bake the tart shell blind for 20 minutes. Remove from the oven and brush the crust with beaten egg white, then let cool.

Trim the rhubarb and chop it into roughly ½-inch slices. Put it in a saucepan with the orange juice and heat briefly, just until the rawness is taken off it. Remove, drain, and keep the liquid.

Beat the egg yolks in a small bowl. In another bowl, mix ⅔ cup sugar with the flour and the melted butter. Then add the yolks and enough of the rhubarb liquid to turn it into a smooth, runny paste. Put the rhubarb into the tart shell and pour the mixture over it. Bake until just set, 20–30 minutes.

Beat the egg whites until they form soft peaks, add ½ cup sugar, and continue to beat until glossy. Then fold in the remaining sugar and the cream of tartar, using a metal spoon. Spoon this over the baked tart to completely cover the fruit, sprinkle with a bit more sugar, and return to the oven for about 15 minutes, until the peaks are bronze-tipped. Nigella likes to eat it cold, but says that for most tastes, 10–12 minutes out of the oven is about right.

Mjuk Toscakaka

Serves 6–8
⅔ cup butter
½ cup sugar
2 eggs
1 tsp pure vanilla extract
1¼ cups all-purpose flour
1 tsp baking powder
5 tbsp water

For the top
¼ cup slivered almonds
4 tbsp butter
5 tbsp sugar
1 tbsp all-purpose flour
1 tbsp milk

Kristina von Wrede is an exceptionally talented home cook. She is Swedish, and lives near me in Somerset, and I know whenever I go to dinner with her and her husband, Fritz, that the food will be original and unlike anything else anybody I know would cook. Organic vegetables and herbs from her walled kitchen garden, her own geese, and wonderful wild boar and venison in the fall from Fritz's family in Westphalia. I have had several birthday dinners with her, and there are always candles lit, a sense of ceremony, roses around the place setting, everything looks simply beautiful. We have had midsummer-eve feasts too, with midnight dancing around the maypole, and celebrated Saint Lucie's Day, Sweden's patron saint, a blind saint for a dark country, with traditional saffronbrod and mulled wine on the shortest night of the year.

I spent a morning there recently, with Kristina making the following three tarts while I watched and took notes in her kitchen. "The Swedes still do a lot of baking even though they've got jobs," Kristina informed me. "And the quality of their flour is very good." Her kitchen constantly smells of baking, homemade breads, cakes, little caraway-seeded rolls, a lot of the ingredients brought back from London's Swedish deli Swedish Affar, or from Ikea.

"This tart is very simple but very effective," Kristina says. "That's what I like about Swedish food. In the old days, a good housewife had to be able to bake seven kinds of cookie before she married. Because the Swedish are still very much a farming people—it was ninety percent in the 19ᵗʰ century—and it is such a big country, they are very particular with their baking. They can't just go down to a local shop."

Preheat the oven to 350°F and butter a 9-inch tart pan.

Cream the butter and sugar together thoroughly in a bowl. Beat in the eggs, little by little, then add the vanilla extract. Sift in the flour and baking powder, beat thoroughly, then add the water and continue beating until smooth. Scrape into the buttered tart pan, smooth the top, and bake for about 30 minutes. Remove from the oven, and turn the temperature up to 400°F.

For the top, put all the ingredients together into a saucepan and heat. Allow to bubble to amalgamate the mixture, then spoon this over the tart and return to the oven to brown for 5 minutes. Don't let it burn. You will have a deliciously fudgy, crunchy top. Serve plain, without cream, warm or cold.

Mjuk Mandeltarta
Soft Almond Tart

There is a delicious organic Dutch marzipan that you can buy from health food shops; get it if you can, some of the more commercial makes are deeply inferior. Or you could make your own.

Serves 8

1½ cups organic marzipan
grated zest and juice
    of 1 orange
3 eggs
2 tbsp all-purpose flour
generous ½ tsp baking
    powder

Preheat the oven to 350°F and butter a 10-inch springform tart pan.

Add the marzipan to the grated orange zest in a bowl, then beat in the eggs. You are aiming for a smooth, unlumpy dough. Add the orange juice and beat with a whisk. Sift the flour and baking powder over the mixture and beat again. Turn the mixture into the buttered pan and bake in the lower third of the oven for 30—40 minutes.

If it rises well, slice it in half and fill it with crème pâtissière, or lemon or orange curd. Otherwise, spread one of these over the top. If you've done the former, you could sift confectioners' sugar over the top, but if you want a more special tart, put some whipped cream on top, and then add some soft fruit— raspberries, loganberries, black currants. Kristina defrosts her own soft fruits if she is making this in the winter, making sure that the juice is properly drained first. Sometimes she adds melted chocolate to the whipped cream, and some finely chopped candied orange.

Ambrosia Kaka

This is like the Toscakaka, but made with the zest and juice of an orange instead of with water, and topped with an orangey glaze.

Serves 6—8

⅔ cup slightly salted butter

½ cup sugar

2 eggs

1¼ cups all-purpose flour

1½ tsp baking powder

grated zest and juice
   of 1 orange

"Vanilkram" filling

2 egg yolks

5 tbsp each heavy cream
   and milk

1 tbsp potato flour,
   or 1½ tbsp cornstarch

1 tbsp sugar

½ a split vanilla bean,
   the middle scraped out

For the top

7½ tbsp confectioners'
   sugar

1½ tbsp orange juice

3 small pieces of
   candied orange,
   cut into tiny cubes

Preheat the oven to 350°F and butter a 9-inch tart pan.

Cream the butter and sugar together thoroughly in a bowl, then add the eggs, one at a time, beating together thoroughly. Sift in the flour and baking powder, beat well, then add the orange zest and 5 tablespoons of juice, and continue beating until smooth. Scrape into the buttered tart pan and bake for 30—40 minutes.

For the *vanilkram*, whip everything together in a saucepan, stirring over gentle heat until thickened. Remove the vanilla bean and let cool.

Once you have removed the tart from the oven, let cool for 15 minutes. Halve it if you like, and fill with *vanilkram*.

For the top, mix together the confectioners' sugar and orange juice, then spread over the tart, and sprinkle with the candied fruit. The result should be a thin glaze, not a thick one.

Sweet Tarts

"This most versatile and perfectly self-contained of foods is without doubt one of the great joys of my cooking life, equally as pleasurable in the making as in the eating."

Roast Fig and Honey Tart with Cointreau (page 112)

PEACH, VANILLA, AND AMARETTI TARTE TATIN

Invention in the culinary world is a difficult and risky thing to define. We are all influenced by so many people, and there is no knowing, when one comes up with something one imagines to be original, whether or not someone else hasn't first—it is more than likely that they have. I am under no illusions about that. However, when I first dreamed up this tart I have to confess I felt really proud of it, and amazed that, first time round, it tasted quite as good as it did. The amber-hued peaches speckled with vanilla and sticky with caramel, and the crust, not overpowered, but brought to life with crushed amaretti, make it something where all the contrasting flavors complement and add, yet the three very different notes remain simple, true. Try it and see.

Serves 8

For the dough

8 amaretti

1½ cups all-purpose flour

6 tbsp unsalted butter, cut
into pieces

2–3 tbsp ice water

For the top

8 ripe peaches (white are the
absolute best, but yellow-
fleshed are fine)

juice of 1 lemon

1 vanilla bean

6 tbsp sugar

4 tbsp unsalted butter

To make the dough, crush the amaretti in a food processor, add the sifted flour and butter, and process briefly to combine, then add 2–3 tbsp ice water and process until the mixture comes together. Wrap in wax paper and chill for at least 20 minutes.

Preheat the oven to 375°F. Roll out the dough ½ inch wider than the circumference of the pan—I use a heavy, 10-inch diameter Cousances enameled cast-iron skillet with a metal handle that I can put in the oven   and set the shell to one side.

Scald the peaches in boiling water for 30 seconds. Peel, and sprinkle them with lemon juice to prevent discoloration.

Split the vanilla bean and scrape it out into the sugar. Warm the sugar in the skillet until it is a deep, dark brown, and totally liquid. Do not stir, but move the pan around to prevent burning. Remove from the heat and dot with half of the butter. Put half a peach in the middle of the sugar mixture, cut side up. Quarter the rest, and, starting at the outside of the pan, lay them next to one another in a tightly packed wheel. Arrange the remaining quarters in an inside wheel. Dot with the rest of the butter and put the pan back over the heat for 2–3 minutes to gently start the cooking.

Remove from the heat, cover with a mantle of pastry that you tuck inside the pan edge, and bake for 25–30 minutes. Remove from the oven and let cool for 10 minutes before inverting onto a plate. Delicious with crème fraîche.

PEAR AND GINGER TARTE TATIN

It is the beginning of November. The first smallish and deceptively bullet-like Conference pears are in the shops, the forecast is for storm-force winds and floods. And I've got George Morley and her husband, Shawn Whiteside, and baby, Charlie, coming to stay. (See her Leek Tart recipe on page 61). George is being the perfect weekend guest and bringing down Friday night's supper from London. I have a sort of sixth sense that it might be worth making a dessert. Other than seven pears, my kitchen cabinets shriek ginger in syrup. Ginger is the great warming herb of Chinese medicine, and feels like the most eligible partner for the cool scentedness of the pear. Turn back to the previous page if you need confidence-bolstering to attempt a tarte tatin; it really, really isn't difficult, any more than a soufflé is, although it is always held up to be.

Serves 8
7 pears
juice of 1 lemon
nearly ⅓ cup vanilla sugar
4 tbsp unsalted butter
ginger syrup and 3 knobs of
    ginger, cut into small dice

Make your pie dough (page 139) with 1½ cups white flour and 6 tablespoons unsalted butter , then chill. Preheat the oven to 350°F and put a baking sheet in to heat. Roll out the dough ½ inch wider than the circumference of the pan; I use my 10-inch cast-iron skillet that I can put in the oven. Set the tart shell aside. Peel, core, and halve the pears; turn them in lemon juice to prevent discoloration.

Warm the sugar in the skillet until it liquifies. The moment the sugar is treacly brown all over but not burned, remove it from the heat, and dot with half the butter; it will bubble up and become absorbed. Then pour over some ginger syrup, a couple of tablespoons or three; any more will be intrusive. Fit the pears head to tail in spokes, sardine style, around the pan. Or, halve the halves vertically into quarters and tuck them on their sides, then cut circular shapes to fill the gaps in the middle, core side up. Sprinkle the ginger pieces over the pears, and then cover the whole in a blanket of dough, tucking it in under the pears around the edges.

Bake on the middle shelf of the oven on the preheated baking sheet for about 30 minutes. The juices should be bubbling stickily away around the edge. Remove from the oven and let cool for about 10 minutes before flipping out onto a plate. The mahogany-tinted pears that gaze up at you should be perfectly cooked and glossily glazed with caramel.

Pass around heavy cream and a bottle of eau de vie de poires if you are lucky enough to have any, and feel the ginger's warming presence as it hits your insides.

A Tatin of Apricots Stuffed with Almond Paste

January, and the memory of summer fruits is just that. When Miranda brought home two Australian girls, over for a schools' field hockey tour, I was determined that they should get something to eat that wasn't entirely sunshine-free. Alighting on a box of apricots, I decided to fill them with a rich frangipane paste, and bake them under a tatin crust.

Serves 8

6 tbsp sugar

¼ cup ground almonds

2 tbsp unsalted butter, cut into small pieces

2 tbsp vanilla sugar

1 egg

a few drops of bitter almond extract (I use Culpeper's)

2–3 dozen fresh apricots

Make your pie dough (page 139) with 1½ cups white flour and 6 tablespoons unsalted butter , then chill. Preheat the oven to 350°F and roll out the dough a little larger than the ovenproof skillet, as before (page 88). Caramelize the sugar in the same pan in which the tart is to be cooked.

Mix the ground almonds, butter, and vanilla sugar with the egg and a few drops of almond extract to make a rich paste. Slice each apricot in half and remove the pits, and then fill the cut halves with the paste. Pack the apricots tightly into the pan, paste side up, in circles, with any left over in a double layer at the center. Tuck a blanket of dough under the edges in the usual way, and bake for 35 minutes. Let it rest for 10 minutes before inverting and serving with crème fraîche.

Lemon Meringue Pie

This is another of those golden age of childhood recipes, and one of the first desserts I learned to cook. My grandmother's cook, Rhoda, steely gray hair in a taut bun, and maroon-flowered dress worn nearly down to her black old maid's shoes, had the lightest touch that pastry ever saw. She always made this when my brother, Daniel, and I went to stay at Upper Parrock, our grandparents' beautiful medieval hilltop house in East Sussex. And she always judged it right. The gloopy lemon filling was never too sweet, never too cornstarched, and the top rose cloud-like, stepped, a breath of weightless meringue with that final, brittle brown top that a spoon had to crunch through before meeting the gooey middle and the smooth, tart lemon. The addition of a few crushed cardamom seeds to the lemon filling robs the dessert of its nursery status, but is well worth the experimentation.

Serves 6

9-inch unbaked tart shell, chilled (page 139)

Lemon filling

grated zest and juice of 3 organic lemons

⅓ cup cornstarch

1¼ cups water

3 large egg yolks

5½ tbsp vanilla sugar

4 tbsp unsalted butter, cut into small pieces

Meringue

3 large egg whites

½ cup vanilla sugar

Preheat the oven to 375°F. Bake the tart shell blind for 15 minutes, then remove the beans, brush the crust with beaten egg white, and return to the oven for 5 minutes. Remove the tart shell from the oven, and turn the heat down to 350°F.

For the filling, put the lemon zest and juice in the top of a double boiler. Add the cornstarch and whisk in 2 tablespoons of the water until you have a smooth paste. Add the remaining water, boiling hot, and keep whisking over simmering water until the mixture is thick and bubbling. Remove from the heat and whip in the yolks, sugar, and butter. Let cool slightly while you make the meringue.

Whip the egg whites until stiff, scatter in one-third of the sugar, and whip again until stiff. Fold in another third of the sugar with a metal spoon. Spread the lemon mixture over the tart shell. Pile the meringue on top and sprinkle it with the remaining sugar. Bake for 15–20 minutes. Let cool slightly, then invert. Best served with thin cream.

Seville Orange and Marmalade Tart

This is a delicious winter dessert for the Seville orange season, or, out of season, you can make it with less sugar, ordinary oranges, and a lemon, or blood oranges if you want an unguessable-looking tart. I once made blood orange and cardamom ice cream to accompany it, which was pink, fragrant, and utterly delicious. Perfect after rich goose, which I always cook on New Year's Eve.

Serves 6 – 8

9-inch unbaked tart shell, chilled (page 139)

2 – 3 tbsp tart orange marmalade

grated zest and juice of 4 Seville oranges

½ cup unsalted butter, softened

1 cup vanilla sugar

4 large eggs, beaten

Preheat the oven to 375°F. Bake the tart shell blind for 15 minutes, then remove the beans, prick the bottom with a fork, brush with beaten egg white, and cook for a further 5 minutes. Remove the tart shell from the oven and turn the heat down to 350°F.

Spread the marmalade over the bottom of the tart. Put the grated orange zest in a bowl. Beat in the butter and sugar, then add the beaten eggs and whip everything together. Place the bowl over a saucepan of simmering water and stir until the mixture has melted and dissolved. Remove from the heat and stir in the orange juice. Pour into the marmalade-lined tart and return to the oven for 20 minutes or so, until barely set. Serve warm, with heavy cream.

Ricotta Tart with Rum-Soaked Golden Raisins

This is surprisingly un-rich, the liquor-soaked golden raisins adding a mellow sharpness, the whipped egg whites a soufflé-like lightness that the children adored. It is phenomenally quick to make, and it cooked while they were tucking into their lasagne. I added chocolate to their tart, turning it into a swirly, marble-topped picture; the grown-ups' I left plain. Let them cool for 15 minutes before inverting them.

Serves 6–8

9-inch unbaked tart shell, chilled (page 139)

2 tbsp dark rum

⅓ cup golden raisins

2 cups ricotta, or just over 1 lb fresh ricotta if you can find it

5 eggs

3 tbsp potato flour

6 tbsp vanilla sugar

1 orange or lemon

2 oz (2 squares) best bitter chocolate

2 oz unsalted butter (optional)

Preheat the oven to 375°F. Bake the tart shell blind for 15 minutes, then remove the beans, and bake for a further 5 minutes. Let cool, and turn the oven down to 350°F.

Heat the rum gently in a small saucepan with the golden raisins and allow them to absorb the liquor. Push the ricotta through a strainer or the smallest holes of your mouli into a large bowl, add one whole egg and the four yolks, and mix thoroughly. Add the potato flour and vanilla sugar. Pour the rum-soaked golden raisins into the ricotta mixture and incorporate. Grate in the citrus zest. Whip the egg whites until stiff, stir one tablespoon into the ricotta mixture, and then lightly fold in the rest. If you are doing the plain version, stop here, and spoon the mixture into your tart shell.

If you are doing the chocolate version, melt the chocolate and butter together over very low heat, then pour lightly over the top of the ricotta mixture, and pour it into the tart shell, minimally disturbing the chocolate with a skewer into marbled swirls.

Bake for 45–50 minutes—it should be set right across, but not rigidly so. Let it sink and cool, and invert after about 20 minutes. I think it should be eaten cold, or at most with a bare memory of warmth.

"The first June strawberries, when not devoured straight from the punnet, are christened in a tart with a voluptuous, vanilla-ey crème pâtissière, in which they have been plunged waist deep and glazed to gloopy perfection."

STRAWBERRY TART

This is the spirit of summer; the first June strawberries, when not devoured straight from the punnet, are christened in a tart with a voluptuous vanilla-ey crème pâtissière, in which they have been plunged waist deep and glazed to gloopy perfection. I cannot understand why anyone could be fearful of making this look as good as the finest French pâtissier. It is nuts and bolts cooking. If you can make dough, the rest's a breeze. If you can't, either learn how to from the dough-making section of this book, or, better still, from watching someone who can, or give this book to someone who'll use it.

All three of my children put it on their top three desserts list, and I think I agree. I confess I always make a hubcap-sized version rather than the normal tart-sized one. This is not because I make it only when people are coming over to lunch or supper, it is because everybody in my family eats gargantuan slices of it, and if there is any left, it is whittled sneakily away on the day. This is not a tart to be served up the following day, tiredly, pinkily soggy; it simply doesn't work. Just eat lots of it.

Serves 8 greedy people
2 lbs strawberries
about 4 tbsp red currant jelly

Crème pâtissière
1¾ cups whole milk
1 vanilla bean, split
4 egg yolks
½ cup sugar
just under ⅓ cup cornstarch

Make a pâte sucrée (page 140) with 1½ cups white flour, 6 tablespoons unsalted butter, 2 dessertspoons confectioners' sugar, 2 egg yolks, and a little ice-cold water; chill for at least an hour. Preheat the oven to 400°F. Line a 12-inch tart pan and bake blind, then remove the beans, and return to the oven for 10 – 15 minutes, until golden and cooked. Watch closely: the edges burn swiftly, and you don't want scorch marks on the bottom. Let cool.

For the crème pâtissière, scald the milk with the vanilla bean and scraped-out grains. Whisk the egg yolks, sugar, and cornstarch together in a bowl, then pour the hot milk onto them and continue whisking. Remove the vanilla bean. Return the mixture to the saucepan and stir over gentle heat until thickened. Pour into a bowl and cool, whipping every so often. When cold, scrape into the tart shell with a rubber spatula. Invert the tart onto a plate or bread board.

Hull the strawberries. Starting at the edge of the tart, stick them upright into the crème pâtissière in a circle and work your way in, using smaller strawberries for each circle. Melt the red currant jelly with a tablespoon of water, then brush it liberally over the strawberries and the custardy gaps. Stand back and admire before you cut it.

Sugar-Topped Raspberry Plate Tart

By late Lenten March, puritanism gets the better of me, and I succumb to unseasonal soft fruit if it's to be found. Raspberries and blueberries this weekend, the former from Spain, so I got to work with a sharp raspberry tart with a last-minute flood of whipped cream and duck-egg yolk funneled into it. I don't know whether there is a consensus as to when a tart becomes a pie, but I think depth is probably the key to it, not crust. This tart has a lid on it, a delicious, brittle, crackly sugar crust of pastry sprinkled with granulated brown sugar, but it is not deep enough to transmogrify into a pie, it is a plate tart. Utterly simple to make, and oozing a confluence of raspberry and ivory juices. In England, if you can bear to wait until June, you can use home-grown raspberries, but I couldn't resist this dress rehearsal.

Serves 6

a little over 1 lb raspberries

generous ⅓ cup vanilla
  sugar

1 egg, separated

about 2 tbsp granulated
  brown sugar

1 cup heavy cream

Make your pie dough (page 139) with 2½ cups organic all-purpose flour and ⅔ cup unsalted butter, and chill. Roll out and use half the dough to line the bottom of a pie plate or shallow, earthenware dish, about 9 inches in diameter. Preheat the oven to 375°F.

Scatter the raspberries over the tart shell with the vanilla sugar. Put the remaining dough on top, crimp the edges with a fork to seal, and brush with lightly beaten egg white. Sprinkle with a thin film of sugar, granulated brown for real crunch, and cut a cross centrally through the pastry lid to let the steam escape. Bake for about 40 minutes.

Do not be alarmed when you see how pallid the crust is; it is not yolked, it is whited. Whisk the cream together with the egg yolk—I had a duck egg—and very gently and slowly pour the mixture through a small funnel down into the hole. This is the only difficult bit; you don't want a flooded crust. Then return it to the oven for 10 minutes. Eat warm or hot; you will not need extra cream.

Brûléed Black Currant or Blueberry Tart

This is a real show-off of a tart, which I started making when my children gave me a blowtorch for Christmas one year. It is still a fantastic thrill aiming a jet of blue flame at the sugary surface and watching the beaded brown bubbles form, crystallize, and turn into a caramelized mahogany sheet. It is just as much of a thrill to crack it, like an egg, with the back of a spoon, and eat the splintery shards of sugar with the strong, tart black currants. If you use blueberries, the cinnamon works equally as well, the result is just milder to the palate, as you would expect.

Serves 6

2½ cups black currants or blueberries

pinch of ground cinnamon

a little light brown sugar

2 large eggs

2 egg yolks

1 cup heavy cream

4 tbsp Kirsch

about 3 tbsp granulated sugar

Make your usual pie dough (page 139) with 1 cup flour and 4 tablespoons butter, adding 1 tablespoon sugar to sweeten it. Chill, then roll out, and line a 9-inch tart pan. Preheat the oven to 375°F. Bake the tart shell blind for 10 minutes, then remove the beans, and bake for a further 10 minutes. Remove the tart shell from the oven and turn the heat down to 350°F.

Put the fruit in a saucepan with 2 tablespoons of water and a pinch of cinnamon, and simmer very briefly. Sweeten to taste with light brown sugar. In a bowl, beat together the eggs, yolks, cream, and Kirsch, and add a little more sugar to taste. Place a single layer of fruit in the tart shell, then pour in the cream mixture, and return to the oven for about 30 minutes, until just firm but with a slightly "sad" center. Let cool.

Just before you want to serve the tart, strew a thin layer of granulated sugar over the top. If you don't have a blowtorch and are going to perform this feat under the broiler, cover the crust edges with a strip of tinfoil, then blast the tart until the sugar bubbles and caramelizes. The thin, burned brown skating-rink top marries beautifully with the creamy, fruity middle.

APPLE TARTS

Apples and pastry. Short, buttery, tart, sugary, the apple tart is one of the greats, has endured changing fashions and seasons, and is as comfortable at the simplest as at the grandest of occasions. A perfect French apple tart, with regiments of fanned, sliced apples, gooey yet slightly burned-edged, with a gloss of strained apricot jam. A glossy, bronzed tarte tatin, dripping caramelized sugar, with a plop of crème fraîche and Calvados. A creamy tart with thick slices of fried apple nestling in the pastry, anointed with egg yolks, cinnamon, and cream.

Even now, in gloomy February, I still have a few sharp-scented baking apples from one of my trees lurking unsullied in a box, rubbing shoulders with one or two blackened neighbors. Paired with some organic Golden Delicious, which I deign to cook with, but not to eat raw, or cooked down and puréed with brown sugar, butter, orange zest, and juice, the apple helps transform this kitchen cabinet month into something more living, less preserved.

This weekend I placed an unevenly rolled oblong of Baker and Spice puff pastry (see page 72) on a floured baking sheet, scoring a rim about an inch or so from the outside edge. Then, leaving the rim clear, I laid peeled, quartered, finely sliced, and overlapping Golden Delicious all the way round, and plonked two baskets of blueberries in the middle in a generous layer. Scattered with sugar, dotted with butter, it was cooked for 10 minutes before I poured a layer of peach jam, melted with a bit of water, but not strained, over the fruit, returning it to the oven for 10 minutes.

We ate the sugary slices in our hands, crisply crusted edges, slightly sogged middles, with the thickened, purply juices bleeding into the apple edges. A recipe? Not quite, but a dessert very definitely, lightly, fruitily satisfying, with no need of cream or spoons. The following recipes are all variations of apple tart, some minimal, some maximal, but all are a delicious end to a meaty or fishy dinner, too fruity to be too rich.

A Plain Apple Tart

Serves 6–8

1 lb crisp, good-flavored
  eating apples—Cox's
  Orange Pippin, Granny
  Smiths, Golden Delicious,
  or what you will
vanilla sugar
apricot jam

Make a pâte sucrée (page 140) with 1 cup flour, 4 tablespoons unsalted butter, 2 tablespoons sugar, and an egg. Chill, then roll out, and line a 9-inch tart pan. Preheat the oven to 350°F.

Peel, core, and quarter the apples, and spread over the tart shell bottom in overlapping, concentric circles, the circles also overlapping. Sprinkle vanilla sugar over the surface and bake for 45 minutes. Brush with warmed apricot jam that you have slackened with a tablespoon of water, but not strained, and return to the oven for 5 minutes. Equally good warm or cold.

Creamy Apple Tart

This creamy, caramelly tart is best made with a tarter eating apple, such as Cox's Orange Pippin. I think a whiff of musky-scented cinnamon enhances the flavor; you might prefer cloves.

Serves 6–8

5 or 6 Cox's Orange Pippin
  apples, peeled, cored,
  and cut into 8 segments
½ cup unsalted butter
¾ cup vanilla sugar
1¼ cups organic heavy
  cream
4 egg yolks
ground cinnamon or cloves
  to taste

Make a pâte sucrée (page 140) with 1 cup flour, 4 tablespoons unsalted butter, 1 tablespoon confectioners' sugar, and 2 egg yolks. Chill, then roll out, and line a 9-inch tart pan. Preheat the oven to 400°F.

Sauté the apple segments gently in the butter, with half the sugar, until half cooked. Remove the apple pieces from the pan and let the sugar caramelize.

Mix together the cream, egg yolks, the remaining sugar, and cinnamon or cloves. Place the cooled apples in tight circles in the tart shell. Pour first the caramel, then the custard mixture, over them, and bake for 35–40 minutes. Serve warm.

NORMANDY APPLE TART

Hot buttered apples, crusted with sugar, are all that is necessary for this deliciously simple tart, made with a crumbly, buttery, biscuity crust.

Serves 6—8

1¼ lbs Cox's Orange Pippin
    or other firm, sweet apples
4 tbsp unsalted butter
3–4 tbsp vanilla sugar, plus
    extra for sprinkling
Calvados

Make a pâte sablée (page 141), chill, then roll out, and line a 9-inch tart pan. Preheat the oven to 400°F.

Peel, core, and thinly slice the apples. Cook them gently with the butter and 3—4 tablespoons of vanilla sugar until golden and translucent, then let cool.

Brush the uncooked tart shell bottom with beaten egg. Place the apples—without their juice, which you have saved separately—in concentric, overlapping circles on the tart shell bottom and cook for 30—35 minutes.

Reheat the buttery juices, with a splosh of Calvados to enhance the Normandy connection, and pour over the tart with a sprinkling of sugar. Return to the oven for a couple of minutes; aim to serve it hot, when, in my opinion, it is at its best.

TARTE TATIN

The perfect autumnal or winter dessert: sticky, bittered caramel clinging to fragrant chunks of apple, and thick buttery dough for the juices to seep into. With a melting lump of clotted cream, this is consoling and warming food of the highest order. Don't let anyone deceive you into thinking it's difficult to flip out of its pan. You just need to start with the right sort of pan. I use a heavy 10-inch diameter Cousances skillet, with a short metal handle that goes in the oven. I also use pie dough, although there are those who use puff pastry. Tarte Tatin was supposedly invented by the Tatin sisters at the Hotel Terminus Tatin near Orléans. History does not relate whether this famous tarte renversée was then made with other fruits in the way everyone does now, even using the principle for savory tarts such as shallot tatins.

Serves 8

6 tbsp vanilla sugar

4 tbsp unsalted butter

8–10 crisp, good-flavored
eating apples

juice of 1 lemon

Make your pie dough or puff pastry in the usual way (see pages 139–141), with 1½ cups flour, and chill while you prepare the apples. Preheat the oven to 350°F.

Put the sugar in the skillet in a thin layer and heat it gently. Watch it all the time, as some bits of your pan will brown before others. You want the sugar to melt to a dark brown liquid all over without burning. On no account stir it, just shake the pan and turn it as you need to redistribute the sugar. Remove from the heat and immediately add tiny bits of butter, about a third of the 4 tablespoons, over the sugar. It will bubble instantly.

Peel and slice all the apples into quarters except one, which you should peel and cut in half. Core them all. Squeeze some lemon juice over them to prevent them from discoloring. Put a half apple, cut side up, in the middle of the pan, then a wheel of quarters around it, tightly packed. Dot with the remaining butter and place over gentle heat on top of the stove to start it cooking. Remove from the heat.

Roll out the dough to a circle just bigger than the skillet. Roll it loosely over your rolling pin and thence use it to blanket the apples. Tuck the pastry down the sides of the pan like bedclothes to seal in all your apples, and bake in the middle of the oven for 25–30 minutes. Remove from the oven and let cool for 10 minutes. Cover the pan with a serving plate and flip the tart over on to it. Any stray fruit can be rearranged. The fruit should look glossily, gloopily burnished.

Tarte aux Pommes

This is a half-puréed, half-sliced apple tart, made with baking apples and enough vanilla to seep through the tart apple taste. This is best made with pâte sucrée, to heighten the sweet-sour divide.

Serves 6–8
2 lbs baking apples
¾–1 cup vanilla sugar
1 vanilla bean, split
   lengthwise

Preheat the oven to 400°F. Make a pâte sucrée (page 140) with 1½ cups flour, 6 tablespoons unsalted butter, 2 dessertspoons confectioners' sugar, and 2 egg yolks. Chill, then roll out, and and line a 9-inch tart pan.

Peel, core, and roughly chop half the apples, and stew them very gently with ½ cup of the sugar, the vanilla bean and its scraped-out seeds, in a covered saucepan until almost puréed. You can then strain them if you wish, or merely let them cool, depending on whether you prefer a coarsely textured or smooth result. Taste for sharpness, and stir in a bit more sugar if you have a wickedly sweet tooth.

When cold, fill the uncooked tart shell with your apple purée. Peel and slice the rest of the apples, and arrange them as artistically as you feel moved to over the purée. Bake for 15 minutes, then sprinkle the surface with as much of the remaining sugar as you feel like, and return to the oven until browned, about 20 minutes.

Hot, with cold pouring cream, this is wonderful, or you could bring a sophisticated note to what is essentially rustic food by making an airily light sabayon with some Calvados or hard cider.

Apple Galette

Each region of Lorraine and Alsace has its own version of quiche, and the name is sometimes used for sweet custard tarts too. Old-fashioned quiche Lorraine was made with yeasted bread dough, and likewise the galette, a deliciously crisped, doughy crust harboring a juice-sodden layer of apples, plums, greengages, apricots, or any scented fruits. You can scatter chopped nuts into the dough and over the fruit if you desire. This is not a dish that will good-temperedly reheat, it is to be eaten straight from the oven, or warm. However, you can keep the fruit and the rolled-out dough in the refrigerator, and finish off the dessert when you need it.

Serves 8

For the dough

1¾ cups strong white organic bread flour

2 tsp active dry yeast

1½ tsp salt

2 eggs

5 tbsp melted unsalted butter

about ⅔ cup water or milk lukewarm

a handful of chopped, toasted nuts— hazelnuts, almonds, or walnuts (optional)

For the top

8 Cox's Orange Pippins, or other firm, sweet apples

⅔ cup unsalted butter

½ cup vanilla sugar

1 tsp ground cinnamon and 1 tsp (optional) ground allspice

⅔ cup heavy cream

1 egg

extra sugar

extra nuts (optional)

First, make the dough. Mix together the flour, yeast, and salt, then add the eggs, butter, and liquid to make a soft, coherent, and unsticky dough. Knead by hand or electrically. Put the dough in a bowl inside a plastic bag and seal tightly, letting the dough double in size for at least an hour.

Turn out and punch down the dough, throwing in a handful of nuts if you feel like it. Lightly oil the bowl, roll the dough in it gently, and seal in a plastic bag for a second rise—30 minutes should be enough this time. Punch down again and refrigerate; this dough will not roll out properly if it isn't chilled, it will shrink back temperamentally each time you attempt to roll it.

It should then be rolled out to about a 12-inch circle and placed on a well-greased baking sheet or pizza plate.

Peel, core, and cut the apples into wedge-like segments. Sauté them in the butter until gently colored, then sprinkle them with the sugar and spice mixture. Let them begin to caramelize, then remove from the heat, and cool to tepid.

If you are using plums or apricots, make a cut along the obvious division of the fruit and put about 1½ lbs of fruit and ¾ cup of sugar in a baking dish with a tablespoon of water. Bake until soft enough to extract the pits.

Preheat the oven to 400°F. Leaving an inch free at the edge, arrange the fruit and juices over the dough, put in a warm place for 20 minutes, then bake for 25 minutes.

Beat the cream, egg, and a little sugar together and pour over as much of it as you can—the edge will have risen slightly. Scatter over the nuts if you are using them and cook until set, roughly 10 minutes.

Apple Crumble Tart

A substantial tart, which you can make with puff or regular pie dough, the kind of dessert you would serve a team of post-game children, or hearty-appetited marrow-chilled grown-ups at a shoot lunch.

Serves 6

6 good, crisp eating apples

½ cup unsalted butter, cut into small pieces

1 cup flour

1 cup nibbed almonds

⅔ cup vanilla sugar

a sprinkling of ground cinnamon or cloves (optional)

Preheat the oven to 375°F. Line a 9-inch tart pan with the dough of your choice.

Peel, core, and thinly slice the apples, and fill the tart shell with them. They will sink during cooking, so don't feel apprehensive if the bottom is piled high. Mix the remaining ingredients together quickly with your fingertips and pour them over the top, flattening it evenly by hand. Cook for 35–40 minutes: a skewer will tell you if the apples are cooked through, and the top should be beautifully browned. Serve with crème fraîche, clotted, or crème crue.

Kirkham's Lancashire Cheese and Apple Tart

The perfect combination of deliciously lactic, crumbly Lancashire cheese with sweet, crisp, eating apple, in a highly unusual tart: it can be served as successfully as a main course as it can as a dessert.

Caerphilly would do if you can't find the superb, traditionally made Lancashire; you want a crumbly lactic cheese with a fruity, acid flavor, not a melting, salty cheese.

Serves 6

4 tbsp unsalted butter

5 large Granny Smith apples, peeled, cored, and sliced

2 onions, thinly sliced

2 cups Kirkham's Lancashire cheese, coarsely grated

2 tsp fresh thyme

salt and pepper

1 small egg, beaten

Make your pie dough (page 139) with 2 cups flour and ½ cup butter, adding a teaspoon of fresh thyme to the mixture. Chill, then divide into two balls, one slightly larger than the other, and roll out thinly. Preheat the oven to 350°F.

Melt the butter in a heavy-bottomed skillet, then add the apples and onions, and cook gently until softened, 15–20 minutes. Remove from the heat and stir in the cheese, thyme, and seasoning, then let cool.

Fit the larger layer of pastry into a 9–10-inch loose-bottomed tart pan or shallow pie plate, then heap on the filling. Cover with the top layer of dough, seal, and crimp the edges, and cut a cross in the middle for the steam to escape through. Brush with beaten egg and cook for 35–40 minutes. Serve warm.

BLACK CURRANT MERINGUE TART

Sharp and sugared, currants, like rhubarb, offset the teeth-shocking sweetness of the light, crunchy meringue. I often make this tart with gooseberries, adding a tablespoon of elderflower cordial after they are cooked in the butter—a gorgeous midsummer dessert, made muscaty with the elderflower.

Serves 6

9-inch unbaked tart shell, chilled (page 139)
4 tbsp unsalted butter
2 tbsp light brown sugar
about 1 lb red, white or black currants, cleaned
2 egg whites
1 egg yolk, beaten
¼ cup vanilla sugar
1 tbsp flour
1 tbsp granulated brown sugar

Preheat the oven to 375°F. Bake the tart shell blind for 15 minutes, then remove the beans, brush the pastry with beaten egg white, and cook for a further 5 minutes. Remove the tart shell from the oven and turn the heat down to 275°F.

Melt the butter in a saucepan, stir in the light brown sugar, and, when it is brown and bubbling, throw in the currants. Cover with a lid and cook for 30 seconds, shaking the pan once or twice. Let cool.

Whisk the egg whites until stiff, then gently fold in the beaten yolk, followed by the sugar and sifted flour together. Fill the tart with the currants, top with the meringue, sprinkle with granulated brown sugar, and cook for about 40 minutes, until palely bronzed and cooked through. Serve warm, with thin pouring cream.

Baked Quince Tart

I planted my quince tree about ten years ago, and finally, three summers ago, saw the first couple of fuzzy-skinned golden quinces hanging bell-like from its branches. The following year there were half a dozen, last fall a grand total of twenty. These golden apples attained mythical status for the Greeks; Paris gave one to Aphrodite, and they have become known as the fruit of love, of marriage, of fertility. The slightly bruised ones I bring indoors, their scent filling the fall air with a promise of spring, of blossom with its heady sweetness. Mixed with apples or pears, the quince's rusty pinkness when cooked transforms its autumnal partners, as it does a soufflé, adding its unique granular texture too.

Turning straight to Jane Grigson's seminal Fruit Book, I came upon her "Quinces baked in the French style". I was captivated by the fact that a baked quince was Sir Isaac Newton's favorite dessert. I puréed the resulting dish, and set them inside a tart fragrant with Septembral mellow fruitfulness.

Serves 6

9-inch unbaked tart shell, chilled (page 139)

4 quinces

1 lemon

6 tbsp unsalted butter

½ cup sugar

2 tbsp heavy cream

4 tbsp granulated brown sugar

2 eggs, separated

Preheat the oven to 375°F.

Peel the quinces and hollow out the cores, not piercing the bottom of the fruit. This is a tedious and frustrating job, but I promise you it's worth it. Sprinkle with lemon juice as you go to arrest discoloration. Stand the quinces upright in a buttered gratin dish.

Cream together the butter, sugar, and heavy cream. Stuff the quinces with this mixture and top each quince with a tablespoon of granulated brown sugar. Bake until tender right the way through when pierced with a skewer.

If this is all too much for you, peel, core, and chop the quinces into good-sized chunks, and cook them in a covered saucepan with the sugar and a little water until tender. Strain off the syrupy juice and purée the quinces with the butter and cream in a food processor. Taste for sweetness, then proceed as below.

Turn the oven up to 450°F. Purée the quinces in a food processor, then stir in the two egg yolks. Whip the whites until stiff, fold them into the quince purée, then spoon the mixture into the uncooked tart shell. Cook for 15 minutes, then turn the heat down to 350°F, and cook for a further 20 minutes. Let cool for about 10 minutes before inverting and serving.

"Slightly bruised quinces I bring indoors,

their scent filling the fall air with a promise of spring,

of blossom with its heady sweetness."

Vanilla and Raspberry Tart

I am writing this at the end of October, slightly disbelievingly. To be able to buy late-cropping Scottish raspberries when even the walnuts and quinces have been squirreled or brought down by the wind, and the last blackberries have vanished from the hedges, is a rare treat. It does not, however, feel quite right to serve them raw, as though it were the memory of a summer lunch. I had been thinking about inventing a vanilla tart, and this seemed the perfect late fall combination. The sharp raspberries, unsugared, bleed a bit and rise to the surface, bright cerise dots that look like unblotted ink, slightly fuzzed into the brilliant yellow background of custard. Six egg yolks give it a powerful color and flavor, with a predominant but not overpowering scent and flavor of vanilla. This is one hell of a rich tart.

Serves 6–8
1¼ cups organic heavy
    cream
½ cup crème fraîche
about 1 cup whole milk
1 vanilla bean, split
6 egg yolks
roughly 3 tbsp vanilla sugar
1–2 tsp vanilla extract
¾ lb raspberries

Preheat the oven to 350°F. A pâte sucrée (page 140) is best, made with 1 cup organic white flour, 4 tablespoons unsalted butter, 1 tablespoon sifted confectioners' sugar, and 2 egg yolks. Chill, then roll out, and line a 9-inch tart pan. Bake blind for 10 minutes, then remove the beans, prick the crust with a fork, brush lightly with egg white, and return to the oven for 5 minutes.

Scald the creams and milk with the vanilla bean and its scraped-out insides. Put the egg yolks into a 3-cup measuring pitcher and whip in 2 tablespoons of the vanilla sugar. Add the vanilla extract, 1 teaspoon to start with. Whip in the scalded creams, taste, and add more vanilla extract if necessary. I like mine strongly, but not overpoweringly, vanilla-ey. Add the last spoon of sugar if you think you need it.

Pull the tart shell half out of the oven and shoot the raspberries onto it in a single, generous layer. Pour in the custard from the pitcher: this is the easiest, quickest way to decant liquid into a tart and ensure it carries on cooking, doesn't go soggy, and doesn't do the dreaded trick of seeping out of the tart shell and anointing the oven. Turn the oven down to 325°F and bake for 40–50 minutes. Check after 40, and if set with a slight wobble, remove and let cool for 15–20 minutes. Turn out and eat warm.

ALMOND CREAM TARTS

Prune, cherry, greengage, plum, nectarine, peach, or apricot, all are delicious sunk slightly into a gooey, almondy middle, laced with a splash of liqueur if you like, the fruit baked slowly in the oven first, yielding its sugary juices for you to pitcher and pour over the finished tart. Kirsch for cherries, Quetsche for plums, and last night, April Fool's Night in the west of Ireland, I substituted Calvados for Armagnac, since I didn't have the latter, and thickly grated some peeled apple into the almond cream, which I covered in baked Agen prunes. The black-velvety fruit had first been soaked in a jar of prune juice. This was a perfect dish to follow chicken from the Westport Country Market, roasted with tarragon and lemon, and finished with cream, butter, the oniony pan juices, and more freshly chopped tarragon.

Serves 6–8

9-inch unbaked tart shell, baked blind (pages 139–140)

about 24 prunes, soaked in water or prune juice to cover, or 15–18 apricots or plums

Almond cream

1 cup ground almonds

½ cup soft brown or vanilla sugar

½ cup unsalted butter, melted

a few drops of Culpeper's bitter almond extract

1 large egg

either 2 tbsp heavy cream, or 1 tbsp cream and 1 tbsp alcohol (as specified in introduction to recipe)

Whatever fruit you choose should be baked in a slow oven, with the liquid it has been soaked in if using prunes. For, say, greengages or plums, split the fruit, pit it, sprinkle it with sugar, and add about ⅔ cup of water. Bake until softened, then remove the fruit with a slotted spoon, and pour the juice into a pitcher.

Preheat the oven to 425°F. For the almond cream, whip together the ground almonds, sugar, melted butter, almond extract, egg, and cream, plus the alcohol if you are using it. Spread the almond cream over the tart shell bottom, arrange a layer of the baked fruit concentrically over the top, and bake until the cream has just set, 25–30 minutes.

You can glaze the tart if you feel like it, with apricot jam for green or golden fruits, and red currant for crimson, purple, or black fruit.

ROAST FIG AND HONEY TART WITH COINTREAU

This is a beauteous and sluttish, Fall of the Roman Empire kind of dessert. It looks extravagant and decadent, and the taste of ripe black figs, honey, and Cointreau is sweet and pure, with the granular feel of the figs' innards to enhance the texture. Even if D. H. Lawrence has rendered you unable to break open a fig without a degree of self-conscious caution, you will be utterly seduced by this simple, sensual tart. Perfect for late summer and fall, a real painterly tart.

Serves 6–8

about 15 figs

about 3 tbsp runny honey
(use good-quality honey,
like Seggiano's chestnut
honey)

2–4 tbsp unsalted butter,
melted and warmed with
1 tbsp Cointreau

Preheat the oven to 400°F. Make a pie dough (page 139) with 1 cup flour and 4 tablespoons unsalted butter, sweetened with 2 tablespoons sugar. Chill, then roll out, and line a 9-inch tart pan. Bake blind for 15 minutes. Remove the beans, prick the pastry with a fork, brush with beaten egg, and return to the oven for a further 10 minutes.

Cut a cross halfway through each fig, squeeze gently, and splay right open, then fit them snugly together in the tart shell. Dribble in the honey, about ½ teaspoon per fig (you could warm it slightly first to make it pour easily), then brush the melted butter and Cointreau mixture liberally over the figs. Return to the oven for 15 minutes. Remove from the oven and glaze the figs with the remainder of the Cointreau mixture. Serve warm with crème fraîche with a touch of Cointreau whipped into it.

Rhubarb and Lemon Cream Tart

A gaudily colored pink and yellow tart, which is perfect for spring; sharp, fresh, with a dusting of confectioners' sugar to add patches of brown when you blowtorch the top. I served this recently after a stickily delicious Osso Buco with its twin accompaniments of risotto Milanese and heavily garlic-spiked gremolata. I used a large tart shell as I had ten to dinner, so adjust accordingly if you need to.

Serves 10

1 lb 6 oz rhubarb, chopped
    into 1-inch chunks
1¼ cups vanilla sugar
2 tbsp water

Lemon cream filling
6 egg yolks and 1 whole egg
½ cup vanilla sugar
grated zest and juice of
    1½ lemons
1½–2 cups heavy cream
the crumbs from a thick slice
    of Madeira cake, or 1 cup
    crumbled ladyfingers
confectioners' sugar

Make a rich pie dough with 1½ cups organic white flour and 6 tablespoons unsalted butter, a generous tablespoon of unrefined sifted confectioners' sugar, the grated zest of an organic lemon, and a whole egg. No water. Just swirl everything together in a food processor until it coheres, then chill in plastic wrap for an hour. Preheat the oven to 400°F. Line a greased 12-inch tart pan with the dough, and bake blind for 10 minutes, then remove the beans, prick the crust with a fork, and bake for a further 5 minutes. Take out of the oven and let cool. Turn the oven down to 325°F.

Cook the rhubarb, sugar, and water together slowly in a covered saucepan until the rhubarb is soft, then tip the contents of the pan into a strainer over a bowl, and leave until the juice has finished dripping through. Reserve both separately.

For the lemon cream filling, beat the yolks and the whole egg with the sugar, lemon zest, and juice, and the cream, then transfer to a pitcher. Put a layer of cake crumbs over the bottom of the tart, and spoon the drained rhubarb on top of them. Put the tart onto a baking sheet in the oven, and then pour the lemon mixture over. This means you do not have to carry a full, slopping tart to the oven. Bake until just set, about 25–30 minutes.

Sprinkle a thin film of confectioners' sugar over the surface and blast it briefly with a blowtorch; alternatively, protect the crust edges with strips of tinfoil and put it under the broiler. Cool, remove from the tart shell, and serve with a pitcher of the rhubarb juice and one of thin cream.

CORONATION DOUCET TART

I will never forget the first time I attempted the Coronation Doucet Tart. It had been served at Henry IV's coronation banquet, an elegant sweetener to the curlews, partridges, rabbits, and small birds that made up the third course. When a great girlfriend, Anne, and I decided to throw a joint medieval birthday party, this honeyed, saffrony crocus-colored tart was a must. We welcomed our guests in our scratchy, hessian, medieval maiden dresses, minstrels played in the gallery above, and a fanfare announced the triumphal arrival of the roasted wild boar, bedecked with bay and apple, and supine on an old wooden door, as it was paraded before the diners. Each couple shared a wooden spoon, a pewter dish, and an invitation so authentic in its language and sealed appearance that one recipient was convinced it was a court summons. The monks, maidens, revelers, jesters, master, and dancing bear then dug into the silky, creamy, soft-centered depths of the Doucet, with its mild yet intoxicating marriage of flavors. A taste from another age, yet the surprise of honey and saffron is somehow shockingly new, timely, brilliant with its clear notes of both sweet and intensely savory.

Serves 6–8

9-inch unbaked tart shell, chilled (page 139)

1½ cups heavy cream

⅓ cup whole milk

a good pinch of saffron threads

1 heaping tbsp runny honey, preferably lavender or chestnut

6 egg yolks

Preheat the oven to 375°F. Bake the tart shell blind for 15 minutes, then remove the beans, prick the bottom with a fork, brush with beaten egg, and return to the oven for 5 minutes. Turn the oven down to 350°F.

Gently bring the cream, milk, saffron, and honey to scalding point. Take off the heat, and allow the saffron to steep in the liquid, stirring it a bit to infuse the color and flavor. Pour over the egg yolks and whip together. You can pour the cream through a strainer, but I am happy to leave the saffron filaments in the finished tart, bleeding their brilliant orange into it. Taste, and add more honey if you need to. Pour into the tart shell and bake until set, but with a seismic shudder at its middle. Start checking after 30 minutes. Eat it warm.

You could serve it with some raspberries strewn with a little sugar and Kirsch alongside it in the summer, but I think you'll find you don't need cream, unless you are an addict.

RHUBARB, HONEY, AND SAFFRON TART

After discovering that saffron had an affinity not just with the savory, but with the sweet, the next experiment was obviously to try it with fruit. Sharp, tart fruits seem to work best, particularly, I suspect, because of the dominant flavor of honey when you compare it to sugar. You can lose the crust altogether, and just make honeyed, fruited, saffrony custards, cooking them gently in little ramekins in the oven in a bain-marie. Rhubarb, gooseberry, or damson are all a sharp foil to the custard, and their sticky, syrupy juices can be poured warm over the top to offset the richness.

If you are using damsons, don't attempt to pit them raw unless you are a complete masochist. Once cooked, use a cherry pitter, and don't worry about them not holding their shape, it's not the point of the dessert.

Serves 6–8

9-inch unbaked tart shell, chilled (page 139)
½ lb rhubarb, gooseberries, or damsons
¼ cup vanilla sugar
a piece of orange peel for the rhubarb, a head of fresh elderflowers, or 1 tbsp of the cordial for gooseberries
a pat of butter
⅔ cup water
1½ cups heavy cream
⅓ cup whole milk
a good pinch of saffron threads
1 heaping tbsp runny honey
6 egg yolks

Preheat the oven to 375°F. Bake the tart shell blind for 15 minutes, then remove the beans, prick the bottom with a fork, brush with beaten egg, and return to the oven for 5 minutes. Turn the oven down to 350°F.

Meanwhile, stew the fruit gently in a covered saucepan together with the sugar, the orange or elderflower flavoring, and the butter and water, until softened. Tip the contents of the pan into a strainer over a bowl, pick out the orange peel or elderflowers, and leave until the juice has completely finished dripping through.

Gently bring the cream, milk, saffron, and honey to scalding point. If the fruit is very sharp, add a bit more honey to the mixture. Take off the heat and allow the saffron to infuse for at least 15 minutes, giving it a gentle stir. Pour over the egg yolks and whip together. Spread the fruit over the cooled tart shell, then pour in the custard, and bake for about 30 minutes, until set with a shudder. Serve warm.

LEMON TART

This is the perfect dessert. I never tire of a state-of-the-art lemon tart. I have eaten and made scores of them, but this, for me, is the utopian version, with just the right sharp, gelled, rich creaminess. Just thinking about it is like putting sherbet on the tongue, instant salivation. I usually scorch the top with confectioners' sugar and my blowtorch, but it is not mandatory. I like it hot, warm, or cold, but I think warm wins by a whisker.

Serves 10
6 lemons
9 egg yolks—this is not
   a misprint!
1½ cups vanilla sugar
1¼ cups heavy cream
3 tbsp sugar for the top

Make a pâte sablée (page 141) with 2 cups all-purpose flour, ¾ cup unsalted butter, ¼ cup sugar and 2 egg yolks. Wrap in waxed paper and chill for an hour. Preheat the oven to 400°F. Roll out the dough and line a 12-inch tart pan—there is something about a lemon tart that prohibits one from making it small. Bake blind for 10 minutes, then remove the beans, and bake for a further 10 minutes.

Meanwhile, finely grate the zest of two lemons, then squeeze the juice of all six and set aside. Whisk together the egg yolks and sugar until thoroughly mixed. Add the lemon juice and zest, and continue whisking, then whip in the cream. Taste, and if it is not quite sweet enough, add a bit more sugar. Transfer the mixture to a pitcher.

As soon as the crust is cooked, reduce the oven temperature to 250°F. Pull the tart half out of the oven and pour the filling into it as high as you dare. Nudge it gently back into the oven and cook for about 30 minutes. The result should be barely set, wobbly, and tremulous; it will go on firming up outside the oven. Remove and let cool for at least 20 minutes.

Scatter a thin layer of sugar over the surface and blowtorch it. If you haven't got one of these magical gadgets, protect the crust with strips of tinfoil and whack the tart under a hot broiler until puddled with brown bubbles. Let cool slightly, even if you want to eat it hot.

Chocolate Tart with Pralinéed Almonds

This is a beautifully rich, chocolatey dessert, smart enough for a good dinner. A flourless and pastryless tart, what a blessed relief—not that it is less rich than a more conventional tart. It bursts into life with some really vanilla-ey ice cream to accompany it, the tart consumed at room temperature with a dollop of cold alongside it.

Serves 10–12

1 cup whole almonds, skinned and chopped

1 tbsp unrefined confectioners' sugar

5 oz (5 squares) of the best bitter chocolate

4 tbsp unsalted butter, cut into small pieces

¼ cup heavy cream

7 egg whites and 5 yolks

½ cup ground almonds

1 heaping tsp ground coffee

½ cup organic cocoa powder

For the top

5 oz (5 squares) of the best bitter chocolate

about ⅓ cup milk

Put the chopped almonds in a gratin dish, throw over a tablespoon of confectioners' sugar, and place under a hot broiler, turning the dish every so often. You want the sugar to dissolve and adhere to the browning nuts. Watch carefully: brown, not black.

Preheat the oven to 350°F. Butter and flour a 12-inch tart pan.

Melt the chocolate in the top of a double boiler. Stir the butter into it, then stir in the cream, and remove from the heat.

In a large bowl, whisk the egg whites until stiff, then gently fold in the yolks, followed by the ground almonds and coffee. Then fold in the chocolate, butter, and cream mixture, and mix gently to incorporate. Pour half the mixture into the tart pan, then add the pralinéed almonds to cover the surface, before pouring on the rest of the mixture. Cook for 15 minutes. Remove from the oven, and let cool slightly before inverting onto a wire rack. Let it become completely cold.

For the top, melt the chocolate and milk together in a double boiler, then spread over the tart. When cool, you could gently sift on a touch more cocoa, but don't be heavy-handed; cocoa is bitter, with seventy percent cocoa solids. I am anti the current trend of dredging everything in confectioners' sugar, which is for sponge cakes as far as I'm concerned, or for brûléed tart tops.

PRUNE, ALMOND, AND ARMAGNAC TART

Always try and find Agen prunes: good health food shops, delis, and supermarkets stock them. Soak them in green gunpowder tea if you can, or smoky Lapsang Souchong as a second choice—it adds a subtly mysterious something to the end result. This is a classic trio, prune, almond, and Armagnac, needing no excuses or tampering with.

Serves 6–8

9-inch unbaked tart shell, chilled (page 139)

4 tbsp heavy cream

2 eggs

½ cup vanilla sugar

1 cup ground almonds

4 tbsp Armagnac

1 tsp bitter almond extract (Culpeper's is good), or try orange flower water

4 tbsp butter

2 cups Agen prunes, soaked and pitted

Preheat the oven to 400°F. Bake the tart shell blind for 10 minutes, then remove the beans, brush the shell with beaten egg, and prick with a fork, then return it to the oven for a further 10 minutes.

In a bowl, whisk together the cream, eggs, sugar, ground almonds, half the Armagnac, and the almond extract. Melt the butter and whip it into the mixture.

Dry the prunes on a paper towel and arrange on the tart shell bottom. Pour the filling over them and bake for about 25 minutes. Sprinkle with the rest of the Armagnac, cool slightly, and serve.

TREACLE TART

Gloopy, gooky, toothachingly sweet treacle tart, with a solid spoonful of clotted cream slipping deliquescent from the slice, turning buttery at the edges as it slides. The ultimate comfort food, to please diehard traditionalist and the young and innocent-palated alike. This version has a softly gelled golden center quite unlike the plain syrup and bread—crumb version, and once you have cooked it, you will no longer think what a cheek I've got for including a recipe for something that everyone knows. Or for telling you that when Julia Roberts comes to stay she drools over it, and busies herself making and twisting the lattice for the top—which is how I usually serve it—all the quicker to cook it with. I associate her with this dish in the way one does when one knows one's friends' favorite dishes, and she deserves a mention every bit as much as the creators in the Other People's Tarts chapter.

I prefer a whole wheat crust for this tart, but please yourself. I find it lessens the impact of the rich sweetness, and a bit of bran is not a bad thing in the circumstances!

Serves 6–8

2 cups light corn syrup

2 tbsp unsalted butter, cut into small cubes

1 large egg, beaten

2–3 tbsp heavy cream

grated zest of 2 organic lemons

4 heaping tbsp brown bread crumbs, preferably granary

Preheat the oven to 375°F. Make your pie dough (page 139) with 1 cup plain or whole wheat flour, or 1½ cups if you are going to add a lattice top. Line a 9-inch tart pan and bake blind for 15 minutes, then remove the beans, prick the bottom, and bake for 5 more minutes. Turn the heat down to 350°F.

Warm the syrup gently, then, off the heat, add the butter, and stir until melted in. Beat together the egg and cream and add to the syrup, with the lemon zest and bread crumbs. Stir to mix evenly, then pour into the tart shell, add a lattice top if you like, and bake for 25–30 minutes. The filling will have set to a gel.

Leave for about 20–30 minutes before serving warm—there is nothing like hot treacle tart for taking the roof off your mouth. Dollop on the clotted cream, then go for a brisk artery-defying walk afterward.

CUSTARD TART

I remember our local baker, known as "Joan's dad," used to make individual custard tarts in little tinfoil cases when I was a child, with a speckledy sprinkling of nutmeg on the primrose surface. Every so often I was allowed "out the back" of the bakery to see him skillfully fielding his wooden paddle into the bread oven to extract batches of loaves and cakes and pies, and the thrill of being offered a tart, a hot meat pie, or an iced bun. I always chose the hot meat pie, with its crisp crust of lardy pastry and its hotly meaty, gravied interior. I have to confess, the custard tart is one of the few things I cannot, as a non-milk drinker, bring myself to eat; although I can appreciate its silky, wobbly depths. It is just too milky for me. Perversely, crème pâtissière isn't. However, labor of love that it is, I recently made one for our wonderful nanny, Gladys, who had looked after the children for nine happy years before her stroke last year. It has always been, like chocolate is for me, her weakness, her most special indulgence. And she knows a good custard tart when she sees one. It was not easy, knowing her to be an expert in the field, and that I'd have to smell the hot milk and contemplate the horror of the skin on top; so, this recipe has not been tested by me, but by an all-time custard tart fiend, who did not pronounce it wanting. When Gladys says something is "all right," you feel as though you've won the Olympics!

Serves 6–8

9-inch unbaked tart shell, chilled (page 139)
1 cup whole milk
1 cup light cream
2 little pieces of nutmeg plus extra for grating
½ stick of cinnamon
2 large eggs
2 egg yolks
¼ cup vanilla sugar
1 tsp orange flower water (optional)

Preheat the oven to 375°F. Bake the tart shell blind for 15 minutes. Remove the beans, prick the bottom with a fork, and brush it with beaten egg before returning it to the oven for 5 minutes. Remove from the oven, and turn the heat down to 325°F.

Put the milk and cream into a saucepan with the nutmeg and cinnamon, and bring to scalding point. Beat the eggs, yolks, and sugar together in a bowl and pour the hot cream and milk on to them, whipping as you go. Remove the mace and cinnamon, and add the orange flower water if you are using it. Pour the mixture into the tart shell and grate a hint of nutmeg over the top. Bake for about 40 minutes; it should be barely set with a faint tremor to it, as it will go on cooking outside the oven. I am reliably informed that it is best eaten warm.

CHOCOLATE PECAN PIE

A good Sunday lunch dessert that children find moreish, particularly with a dollop of rich, vanilla-speckled ice cream on top.

Serves 6–8

9-inch unbaked tart shell, chilled (page 139)

1 cup light brown sugar

1¼ cups heavy cream

2½ oz (2½ squares) of the best bitter chocolate, broken into pieces

2 egg yolks

a few drops of pure vanilla extract

1 cup pecan nuts, coarsely chopped

Preheat the oven to 375°F. Bake the tart shell blind for 15 minutes. Remove the beans, prick the bottom with a fork, and brush with beaten egg white before returning it to the oven for 5 minutes. Remove from the oven and let it beome cold.

In a double boiler, dissolve the sugar in the cream; before it is boiling, stir in the broken chocolate. Beat the egg yolks in gently with a balloon whisk, and carry on whipping until the mixture has thickened. Remove from the heat, and stir in the vanilla extract and the nuts, then pour the mixture into the tart shell. Cool, then chill until set.

Apricot Tart

A glazed apricot tart with the tops of the fruit lusciously burned, sharpness offset by sugar or crème pâtissière, is a great summer treat and beautiful to behold. I also favor this version, with the added bite of sour cream, and a sweetly syrupy glaze.

Serves 6—8

9-inch unbaked tart shell, chilled (page 139)

about 17 or 18 apricots, halved and pitted

syrup made with 1¼ cups vanilla sugar and 2 cups water

½ cup sour cream

¾ cup heavy cream

2 eggs

sugar

4 tbsp unsalted butter

Preheat the oven to 400°F. Bake the tart shell blind for 15 minutes, then remove the beans, prick the bottom with a fork, and brush it with beaten egg white, and cook for a further 5 minutes. Turn the oven up to 425°F.

Poach the apricots gently in the syrup until barely tender and still holding their shape. Drain and reserve the liquid. Beat the sour and heavy cream with the eggs, and sweeten to taste. Melt the butter and pour it straight into the cream mixture, stirring it in.

Place the apricots cut side up in the tart shell, starting at the edge and working in circles, slightly overlapping. Put the tart shell on the oven shelf, half out of the oven, then pour the custard in from a pitcher. Bake until tremblingly set and browned, about 20—25 minutes. Remove from the oven, and let cool slightly.

Meanwhile, boil down the apricot poaching syrup to make a glaze, which you can brush on just before you are ready to eat the tart.

BAKEWELL TART

My grandmother's cook, Rhoda, never lost her touch at the stove, even after parting company with her memory. Unashamedly old-fashioned English desserts and tarts—Bakewell, lemon meringue, treacle—appeared at the table alongside the Georgian silver cow creamers, the cream coming from my grandparents' farm.

When Rhoda finally relinquished her position and hung up her apron, well into her seventies, Mrs. Pollard, the gardener's wife, took over. Her pastry had just the same crisp crumbliness and lightness of touch. Bakewell tart remains one of the great tastes of childhood. It is a recipe that should be left fearlessly alone, although that has become something daring, almost heretical, in these times of modern twists and fusions. To my mind, it should be considered just as modish to cook with conviction a dish that has fallen from culinary grace, and bring it back into the fold of the repertoire. I do offer an alternative version too, but it abides by the same principles of the original, with its searingly intense raspberry jam lurking under a gooey, scented frangipane crust.

Although Jane Grigson, in her seminal English Food, *assures us that only commercially made Bakewell tarts contain almonds, I think that, rather like the organic nature of the English language, certain things become absorbed into the culinary landscape to a point at which a new generation of cooks no longer questions their etymology.*

Serves 8

9-inch unbaked tart shell, chilled (page 139)

½ cup really good raspberry jam; strawberry is good too

½ cup unsalted butter

½ cup vanilla sugar

1 cup ground almonds

4 egg yolks and 3 egg whites

1 tsp bitter almond extract (I use Culpeper's)

a handful of slivered almonds

Preheat the oven to 400°F. Spread a layer of the jam generously over the tart shell bottom.

Melt the butter until it smells nutty. Whip together the sugar, ground almonds, egg yolks, and whites, and almond extract, then pour the hot butter in, and whip to amalgamate. Pour this over the jam and bake until lightly browned and just set, about 30 minutes. After 25 minutes, strew the slivered almonds over the top of the tart, so they get a chance to brown slightly. A tart to be eaten 10 minutes after it comes out of the oven, still hot, with cold, thin cream poured over it.

Hazelnut and Apricot Tart

This is my variation on the classic Bakewell theme. If you can't be bothered with the Hunza apricots, just use the absolute best apricot jam, but the real thing does make a difference.

Serves 8

9-inch unbaked tart shell, chilled (page 139)

½ lb Hunza apricots, soaked until soft in apple juice, then stewed, pitted, and puréed

½ cup unsalted butter

4 egg yolks and 3 whites

6 tbsp vanilla sugar

1 cup ground hazelnuts

cream (optional)

Preheat the oven to 400°F. Spread the puréed apricots over the tart shell bottom.

Melt the butter until it is golden brown. Beat the egg yolks and whites together with the sugar. Stir in the melted butter, then the ground hazelnuts. The mixture should be dropping consistency—if it doesn't feel quite slack enough you could whip in a little light cream. Pour into the tart shell and bake for about 30 minutes, until the filling is set. Serve hot or warm.

Butterscotch Tart

I first ate this wonderfully melting, gooey tart at Old Head Hotel in the west of Ireland. Staying up for dinner was a novelty in itself, but this became one of the great childhood culinary memories, and remained so until I finally prized the recipe from the cook years later. The meringue was always put onto the top in sculpted serving spoonfuls, one per person, but we never stopped at one helping. How many hotels are there now where you can go back for more, indeed, are encouraged to do so? I came up with a richer version than the original, using cream rather than milk, and darkly damp brown sugar, otherwise it's the same dessert we raved over 30 years ago.

Serves 6–7

9-inch unbaked tart shell made with whole wheat flour, chilled (page 139)

Butterscotch filling

1 cup dark brown sugar

1 cup light cream

6 tbsp butter

½ cup cornstarch, sifted

3 egg yolks

1 tsp pure vanilla extract

Meringue

3 egg whites

¼ cup sugar

Preheat the oven to 375°F. Bake the tart shell blind for 15 minutes, then remove the beans, prick the bottom with a fork, brush with beaten egg white, and return to the oven for 10 minutes. Turn the heat down to 350°F.

Put all the ingredients for the filling in the top of a double boiler and whip together over low heat until thick, creamy, and lump-free. Then scrape the filling into the tart shell.

For the meringue, whip the egg whites until stiff, add one third of the sugar, and whip again. Add another third of the sugar, and fold it in gently with a metal spoon. Either spread the meringue over the filling, or mold it into six or seven quenelle-shaped portions with two large spoons. Sprinkle the remaining sugar over the top and return to the oven for about 20 minutes, or until beautifully browned and crunchy on top.

CANADIAN PIE

Another winner from our childhood summers at Old Head Hotel in County Mayo. This was my father's and my brother Daniel's favorite, and I never managed to purloin the recipe from the cook, so after more error than trial, this is its closest approximation. Its honeyed, curranty sweetness is divine, not at all Christmasy, surprisingly enough, and perfect after a day facing the Atlantic breakers or climbing a mountain.

Serves 6

9-inch unbaked tart shell, chilled (page 139)

4 heaping tbsp light corn syrup

1½ tbsp runny honey

2 tbsp unsalted butter

1 egg, beaten

2–3 tbsp heavy cream

1¼ cups currants

¼ cup ground almonds

¼–½ tsp apple pie spice

¼ tsp grated nutmeg

grated zest of 1 lemon

3 tsp lemon juice

Preheat the oven to 375°F. Bake the tart shell blind for 15 minutes, then remove the beans, prick the bottom with a fork, and brush with beaten egg, and return to the oven for 5 minutes.

Heat the light corn syrup, honey, and butter in a saucepan until liquid. Remove from the heat, and stir in the beaten egg and the cream. Mix all the other filling ingredients together in a bowl, pour in the light corn syrup mixture, and stir well. Pour into the tart shell and cook for about 25 minutes, until nicely puffed up and browned. Serve with cream.

BLACK-BOTTOM CREAM PIE

I came across this irresistible-sounding tart one blissful morning browsing in Kitchen Arts and Letters, Nach Waxman's wonderful cookbook shop in New York. Needless to say, it has its roots in the Deep South, and the legendary James Beard believed the first recipes for it were around the turn of the century. Its chocolate crumb crust is covered by a layer of darkly delicious chocolate pastry cream, signifying the black, swampy lowlands found along the Mississippi River. A froth of rum-flavored chiffon tops this incontrovertibly old-fashioned dessert.

Serves 6–8

Chocolate pastry cream

4 egg yolks

6 tbsp unrefined sugar

4 tsp cornstarch

2 cups scalded milk

1 tbsp dark rum

1 vanilla bean, split

2 oz (2 squares) best bitter chocolate, broken into small pieces

Meringue chiffon topping

1½ tsp gelatin

½ cup heavy cream, whipped

2 tbsp dark rum

1 tsp vanilla extract

3 egg whites

6 tbsp unrefined confectioners' sugar

½ tsp cream of tartar

Make your chocolate crumb crust in the same way as for the White Chocolate Tart with Raspberries (see next page), with 3 teaspoons of organic cocoa added to the dough. Bake it blind for 20 minutes, then remove the beans, prick the pastry with a fork, and brush with beaten egg white before returning to the oven for a further 10 minutes. Let cool.

For the chocolate pastry cream, whip the yolks and sugar together thoroughly, until pale gold, then sift in the cornstarch, and blend until smooth. Whip in the hot milk, then stir the mixture in a saucepan over gentle heat until thickened. Add the rum and the scraped-out insides of the vanilla bean, then add the broken chocolate, and stir until melted and smooth. Scrape the chocolate cream into the tart shell.

For the topping, dissolve the gelatin in 2 tablespoons water, then add it to ½ inch of simmering water in a small saucepan, and dissolve fully over gentle heat for about 3–5 minutes. Stir into the whipped cream and blend thoroughly, add the rum and vanilla, then cool over ice or briefly in the freezer, until it is thickened, but not too cool.

For the meringue, whip the egg whites until stiff, add one third of the sugar, and whip again. Add another third of the sugar and the cream of tartar, and whip until glossy. Fold the remaining sugar in gently with a metal spoon, then fold the meringue into the gelatin mixture, and put on top of the tart. Refrigerate for a couple of hours if possible.

You can decorate with grated chocolate or cocoa powder if the spirit moves you. It is so sublimely rich, you might as well take it as far as you can!

WHITE CHOCOLATE TART WITH RASPBERRIES

*I first cooked this tart at the end of October, when there was an unexpected and welcome
supply of late Scottish raspberries. It made fall recede temporarily, and then I couldn't resist
cooking it again for a Boxing Day lunch party with my friend Brigid. We'd all been asked to
bring a dish, and I happened upon some Third World flown-in berries, which it was worth
abandoning seasonal principles for. I also took a Crème Brûlée Tart (page 136). White tarts
are somehow fitting colors for Christmas food, particularly when they look like thick snow on
top. I am not, on the whole, a flavored-pastry person, but Christmas brings on the
aforementioned abandon, and a dark chocolatey crust made with Green and Black's organic
cocoa is a delightful exception, and a contrast to the acre of white ice-rink topping it.*

Serves 6–8

For the dough

1 cup all-purpose flour

2 tsp organic cocoa powder

2 heaping tsp unrefined
confectioners' sugar

4 tbsp cold butter, cut into
small pieces

1 egg yolk

ice water

For the filling

1 cup crème fraîche

1 cup heavy cream

6 oz (6 squares) organic
white chocolate

½ lb fresh raspberries

Preheat the oven to 400°F. Grease a 9-inch tart pan.

For the dough, sift the flour, cocoa, and sugar into the bowl of your food
processor, add the cold butter, and whiz briefly. Add the egg yolk, and a tablespoon
or two of ice-cold water, and process again just to the point at which it coheres.
Wrap in plastic wrap and refrigerate for half an hour. Roll out on some flour sifted
with a bit more cocoa, and line the tart pan. Bake blind for 20 minutes, then
remove the beans, and cook for a further 10 minutes. It should be crisp and
browned slightly. Let cool.

For the filling, heat the crème fraîche with ½ cup of the heavy cream. Break the
chocolate into a bowl, pour the hot cream over it, and leave for a minute, then stir
until the chocolate dissolves. Cover with plastic wrap with some air holes punched
in it, and put in the refrigerator for 2–3 hours.

Very lightly crush the raspberries with a fork, just to let the juice run a little
(they should remain whole), and put them in a single layer on the tart shell bottom.
Whip the remaining ⅔ cup of heavy cream until thick but still soft, not rigid, and
fold it into the chocolate mixture. Smooth it over the raspberry bottom with a
rubber spatula, and refrigerate for at least another hour. Eat cold.

CRÈME BRÛLÉE TART

Similarly to the White Chocolate Tart with Raspberries on the previous page, I made a dark cocoa crust for this tart. You can, of course, omit the cocoa and make a sweet pie dough instead. Cook the tart shell as in the previous recipe, and let cool.

Serves 6—8

6 egg yolks

2 tbsp vanilla sugar

2 cups heavy cream

1 vanilla bean, split

3—4 tbsp unrefined confectioners' sugar

Beat the egg yolks with 2 tablespoons of sugar, then continue to beat over a double boiler, making sure the pan doesn't touch the boiling water, until thickened and leaving a trail on the beaters. Scald the cream with the vanilla bean and its scooped-out seeds in a saucepan, then whip the cream into the egg and sugar mixture over the heat and stir with a wooden spoon until thickened, 5—7 minutes. Pour through a strainer into a bowl and let cool, then pour into the tart shell and refrigerate for 3—4 hours.

Sprinkle 1—2 tablespoons of the confectioners' sugar over the surface, then blowtorch until melted, or, protecting the crust with strips of tinfoil, place the tart under a hot broiler. Sprinkle over the same amount of sugar again, and continue until browned and bubbling. You will now have a glaze of caramel crackling. Put the tart in the refrigerator and chill for 20—30 minutes before serving.

CRANBERRY TART

The delight of a December fruit tart, scarlet and latticed, at the time of year when everything is dried, preserved, and pickled, is distinctly elevating to the spirits, particularly a tart of such simplicity that you can knock it up when you are making cranberry sauce, one of the seriously satisfying parts of the culinary marathon. I always delight in the crimson berries popping like bubble wrap or bladder wrack in the pan. At this time of year I often add peanuts or grated orange or lemon zest to my dough, although I am not normally given to this practice; in this case, almonds are best.

Serves 6–8

3½ cups cranberries

1 orange

¾ cup light brown sugar

1 cup mascarpone or cream cheese

1 small egg, beaten

Make a pie dough in the normal way (page 139), but using 1 cup each flour and almonds, and ½ cup butter. Chill, then roll out, and line a 9 inch tart pan, and cut or pinking-shear strips of dough for the lattice top. Chill the tart shell for at least 30 minutes. Preheat the oven to 375°F.

Put the cranberries in a saucepan and squeeze enough orange juice over them to almost cover. Simmer, uncovered, until the berries have all popped and you have a thickly bubbling red brew. Add most of the brown sugar, stirring it in and tasting for sweetness; add a little more if necessary.

Stir half the mixture into 1 cup of strained mascarpone or cream cheese. Spread this over the tart shell, then cover with the remainder of the cranberry mixture. Decorate with the pastry lattice, brush with beaten egg, and bake for about 35 minutes. It's best eaten warm.

MASTERING DOUGH

Just as the golden rule for house buying is location, location, location, so for tart dough it is cold, cold, cold. Your butter should be chilled, your hands cold, and if you have a cold marble slab to roll it out on, so much the better. I have even grated butter straight from the freezer when there has been none to be found in the refrigerator. Warmth and overworking are the enemy to the good, buttery-crisp pastry crust. I make my dough in a food processor, and stop the button the moment the flour and butter have cohered into a ball, otherwise the results will be a cross between Play—Doh and underpants elastic. Beware, but don't be frightened. Too wet or too dry, it can, like curdled mayonnaise, be rescued.

Pie Dough

The simplest dough of all. I use 1 cup plain white (preferably organic) or whole wheat flour to 4 tablespoons unsalted butter for my 9-inch tart pan, and 1½ cups flour to 6 tablespoons butter for a 12-inch pan. Rolled out thinly, these quantities fit perfectly. I would also use the smaller quantity for an 8-inch pan, in which case there will be a bit left over.

I sift the flour and a pinch of sea salt into the food processor, then cut the cold butter into small pieces on top of it. I process it for about 20—30 seconds, then add ice-cold water through the top, a tablespoon at a time—about 2—2½ should do it—with the machine running. If the paste is still in crumby little bits after a minute or two, add a tablespoon more of water, but remember, the more water you use, the more the crust will shrink if you bake it blind. One solution is to use a bit of cream or egg yolk instead of water. The moment it has cohered into a ball, stop, remove it, wrap it in plastic wrap, and refrigerate it for at least 30 minutes.

If you are making dough by hand, sift the flour into a large bowl with the salt, add the chopped butter, and work as briskly as you can to rub the fat into the flour with the tips of your fingers only, rather like running grains of hot sand through your fingers. Add the water bit by bit as above; wrap, and chill the dough.

Then scatter a bit of flour on your marble top, roll your rolling pin in it, dust the palms of your hands, and start rolling. Always roll away from yourself, turning the dough as you go, and keep the rolling pin and the marble floured to prevent sticking. Once it is rolled out, slip the rolling pin under the top third of the dough,

and pick it up, judging where to lie it in the greased pan. Never stretch it—it will shrink back. Try to leave at least 30 minutes for the unbaked tart shell to commune with the inside of your refrigerator. Or put it in the night before you need it.

Baking blind

If you are baking your tart shell blind, you will need to preheat the oven to 375–400°F. Some recipes also tell you to put a baking sheet in the oven to heat up. This can be invaluable if you are using a porcelain or other non-metal tart dish, as the hot baking sheet gives it an initial burst of heat to crisp up the bottom of the tart shell. I know that some cooks will be shocked that I could even think of using anything other than metal, but, as well as the aesthetic advantage when it comes to serving, china dishes are guaranteed never to discolor the crust in the way that some metal ones do. Secondly, if you are using a tart pan with a removable bottom (my preference, as they are by far the easiest to invert), placing the tart pan on a baking sheet makes it easier to slide in and out of the oven.

Tear off a piece of waxed paper a little larger than the tart pan and place it over the shell. Cover the paper with a layer of dried beans; the idea is to prevent the shell from rising up in the oven. When the crust is nearly cooked (the timing depends on the rest of the recipe), remove the paper and beans, and prick the bottom of the shell to let out trapped air that would otherwise bubble up. Return the tart to the oven for about 5–10 minutes to dry the tart shell bottom.

Glazing

Brushing the partly baked tart shell with a light coating of beaten egg or egg white ensures a crisp finished tart.

Pâte Sucrée

This dough, enriched with egg yolks, is perfect for summer fruit and chocolate tarts. I normally make it like a basic pie dough, with 1 cup flour to 4 tablespoons butter, adding a tablespoon of confectioners' sugar, and using 2 egg yolks instead of the water. It is even more important to chill this dough thoroughly.

Pâte sablée ("sandy pastry") is even sweeter, and crumbly, like a buttery biscuit. I use 1½ cups flour to ½ cup butter, ½ cup confectioners' sugar, and 2 egg yolks. I put the butter, sugar, and egg yolks into the food processor and work them together quickly, then blend in the sifted flour, and work it into a paste. This needs longer chilling, a minimum of an hour.

Puff Pastry

The richest, lightest leaves of buttery pastry, but it does take time, because of the resting time between each working of the dough. I refuse to compromise over the butter question: commercial brands made with inferior fats are just not what puff pastry is all about. I often buy it ready-made from Baker and Spice (see page 72). In the USA, it is available from Dufour Pastry Kitchen Inc., 25 Ninth Avenue, New York, NY 10014, Tel: 212–929– 2900. They have an overnight delivery service: three 14-ounce packs of chilled pastry cost $52.

1½ cups all-purpose flour
a pinch of salt
¾ cup unsalted butter
about ⅔ cup cold water

Sift the flour and salt into a mixing bowl, then rub in 2 tablespoons of the butter, as for a basic pie dough, or use the food processor. Mix in the water and then gently knead the dough on a floured surface, preferably marble. Wrap it in plastic wrap and refrigerate for 30 minutes.

Keep the rest of the butter out to soften, then flatten it into a 1-inch thick rectangle. On a lightly floured surface, roll out the dough into a rectangle three times the length and 1 inch wider than the rectangle of butter. Place the butter in the center of the pastry and then fold over the top and bottom of the pastry to cover the butter. With the rolling pin, press down on the edges to seal in the butter, then give the dough a quarter-turn clockwise. Now roll the dough out so that it returns to its original length. Fold over the ends again, press them together with the rolling pin, and give a further quarter-turn clockwise. Repeat the process once more, then rest the dough in the refrigerator for at least 30 minutes, remembering which way it is facing.

Repeat the rolling and turning process twice more, then refrigerate for a final 30 minutes before using or freezing. If it gets warm and buttery at any stage during the process, put it in the refrigerator to chill.

INDEX

ACKNOWLEDGMENTS

It is now the Year of the Dragon; it has just been the Year of the Tart. This is how it all began. I telephoned Agent George— Georgina Capel— who is always first in these matters, with the idea for the book. Her enthusiasm is legendary, if that is what she feels about the subject, and in this case, it was. She is not just the deal-maker, contract broker, high priestess of the proceedings, she is friend, cheerleader, and adviser. As a non-obsessive cook, she is invaluable to the process. If she finds the writing of some of the recipes wanting, then she is right. I am, after all, writing for the "home cook," a term which I take to mean everything from the keen and clueless to the off-duty professional. When I suggested to her that the cover might be off-putting to the "keen but clueless" constituent, might look like unattainable restaurant food, she told me she'd immediately thought "I could do that," and, better still, it had made her want to eat it instantly. So it stuck. Without George's support and enthusiasm, all things would be more difficult.

If you don't like the layout of this book, I imagine you are reading it because someone bought it for you. To me, the design is as integral to the look and feel of a good book as the text, and Lucy Holmes, who has designed this, and David Rowley, the art director, have been instrumental in realizing the full picture, and in making sure that the text and the look are so well married that they feel just right for each other. They have accomplished this to perfection.

Maggie Ramsay has had the onerous task of keeping me, my measurements, my textual shortcomings—and longcomings —under strict control. She has done this with constant good humor, precision, questioning, and advice, for which I am hugely grateful.

Michael Dover, as publisher, is the man who can decide whether tarts fit into the overall scheme of things, whether they are a delicious, must-have addition to his list, or not; and luckily, in his wisdom, they were listworthy. I have yet to make him a tart, but now he can choose from *my* list, and he has a deal.

Susan Haynes is rather more difficult to categorize vis-à-vis this book, since she ended up playing rather more roles than she had bargained for. We had begun to get to know each other when we worked together on my last cookbook, *West of Ireland Summers*. This time, unfortunately for Susan, distance, in the shape of the Irish Sea, couldn't keep us apart. Once I'd decided to play home economist, and Susan had worked out my schedule, which included a manic eleven-tart day photographing material that was going to the Frankfurt Book Fair, it was quite clear to me, if not to her, that she would end up elbow deep in the Marigolds if I were to accomplish this ridiculously implausible feat. Without Susan, and my wonderful eldest daughter, Miranda, an accomplished cook and sous chef at seventeen, eleven tarts in a day would have been whatever superlative you care to think of that goes further than impossible. It also goes to show how much more you learn about somebody in one day as part of your kitchen cabinet than you do after any amount of jolly lunches and meetings. Susan is someone whose temperature gauge remains, barometer-like, set fair, whatever the heat in the kitchen, and outside it, right through the last-minute uncertainties and problems that are bedfellows of the impending deadline. Thanks in Imperial measure.

The "Other People's Tarts" chapter suggested itself very early on in the writing, not least because I looked to others for enlightenment and inspiration. I was also doing quite a lot of interviewing at the time, and it seemed crazy not to pick the culinary brains of the first-rate cooks I was writing about. And of the friends who just shared a passion for a really great tart. So I would like to thank all of you for your generosity in giving me such wonderful recipes.

David Loftus has an eye for light, composition, reportage, vérité, and an elegance that is devoid of trickery and fuss. He is as sensitive a portrait photographer as he is with still lifes. It is not as simple as it might appear to shoot a whole book of tarts, with each photograph original, different, true, and so earthily real that you feel you could eat the page. Without David, this book would not be beautiful.

The dedication is to my great friend Janie, whose friendship has been a constant for 21 years, and with whom I have shared most of the great pleasures of life: children, food, wine, films, books, theater, music, Ireland, good conversation. In her inimitably unbossy, understated way, she is responsible for nudging me deeper into the profession of food writing than I would ever have dared to go. David and I took over her kitchen for the photographing of the book, the main memory of which is Janie returning every evening unfazed by the scene of casual devastation, the broken plates—the best one came from Divertimenti, who kindly lent me several beauties—and keener to sample that day's offerings than to have her kitchen back in its original shape and form. Her reaction, on being told that the book was being dedicated to her, was characteristic: "I'm not quite sure what it says about me that the only book that's ever been dedicated to me is about tarts."

It has been a real pleasure to work with all the talented people involved. I hope they enjoy the fruits—and savories— of their labors.
Tamasin Day-Lewis